Daniel Clarke Eddy

Eddy's ttravels in Asia and Africa

Daniel Clarke Eddy

Eddy's ttravels in Asia and Africa

ISBN/EAN: 9783744757744

Printed in Europe, USA, Canada, Australia, Japan

Cover: Foto ©Andreas Hilbeck / pixelio.de

More available books at **www.hansebooks.com**

BY

REV. D. C. EDDY,

AUTHOR OF

"WALTER'S TOUR IN THE EAST"
"TRAVELS IN EUROPE"

BOSTON.
CHARLES E. BROWN & CO.

TABLE OF CONTENTS.

                                                                                                        PAGE

IN MOROCCO 9

    Things at Home. — Malta. — Tangier. — Cape Malabet. — Fez —Morocco. — Manufactures. — Mogadore.

IN ALGERIA 33

    The Pirates. — The Guide. — As-amar. — Rabuat.— Constantia. — Startling Adventures. — Illness.

IN TUNIS AND TRIPOLI 39

    City of Tunis. — Roman Remains. — The Caravansary. — The Servant in Trouble. — Our Hostess.

IN ALEXANDRIA 45

    The Coast. — Alexandria. — Donkey Boys. — The Hotel. — Blindness. — Flies. — Pompey's Pillar. — Cleopatra's Needles. — The Catacombs.

IN ASIA MINOR 62

    New Friends. — Jaffa. — Ramlah. — Smyrna. — Ephesus. — Diana. — Pergamos. — Laodicea. — Sardis. — Philadelphia. — Thyatira. — Nineveh. — Babylon.

IN DAMASCUS 98

    First View. — Mahomet. — Abana and Pharpar. — Antiquity. — Straight Street.— Maronite Quarter. — Dangers. — Flight.

IN GALILEE 111

    Chorazin.— Magdala.— Tiberias.— Sea of Galilee.— Mount Tabor.— Nazareth. — Synagogue.— Safet.

IN SAMARIA 122

    Samaria. — Esdraelon. — Battle of Mount Tabor. — Ebal. — Gerizim. — Jacob's Well. — Nablous. — Sebastia. — Shiloh. — Adventures with the People.

CONTENTS.

IN JERUSALEM	137

An Evening with the Boys. — Jerusalem. — Camps. — A Week around the City. — Gihon. — Siloam. — The Gates. — Via Dolorosa. — Church of the Sepulchre. — Church of the Armenians. — Olivet. — The Temple Area. — Scripture Scenes.

IN JERICHO 165

Consultation. — Long Ride. — The Camp. — Dancing Girls. — The Jordan. — Greek Bathing Place.

IN BETHLEHEM 179

The Dead Sea. — The Town. — Church of Nativity. — Mar Saba. — Convent Life. — The Milk Grotto. — Bible Illustrations. — Shepherds.

IN HEBRON 200

Cave of Adullam. — Cave of Machpelah. — Glass Works. — Productions of the Section. — Prince of Wales. — Dean Stanley.

IN EGYPT 207

The Desert. — Sinai. — Suez. — Cairo. — Pyramids. — The Sphinx. — Heliopolis. — The Nile. — Donkey riding. — Street Scenes. — Funeral Scenes. — Wedding Ceremonies. — Customs of the People. — Government. — Mohammed Ali. — The Mamelukes. — Emin Bey. — Joseph's Well. — Old Tree. — Nilometer. — Cheops. — Dashoor. — Memphis. — Thebes. — Karnac.

IN SOUTHERN AFRICA 253

Ipsamboul. — Birds of the Nile. — Fish of the Nile. — Monsters of the Nile. — Nubia. — Zanzibar. — Madagascar. — City Life. — The Interior. — Changes.

IN INDIA 269

Ceylon. — Colombo. — Kandy. — Madras. — Buddha. — Tanjore. — Travelling in India. — The Thugs. — William Carey. — Henry Martyn. — The Himalayas. — East India Company. — The Punjaub. — Agra.

LIST OF ILLUSTRATIONS.

	PAGE
Entrance to the Khan El-Khalil, *Frontispiece.*	
The Memorial Well at Cawnpore, *Title Page.*	
Crossing the River	9
St. Paul's Bay, Malta	14
Rip Van Winkle Taking a Ride	15
View of Tangier	18
Fish Merchants	20
Serpent Charmers	23
In the Interior	25
Mode of Transportation	27
Costumes in Morocco	29
Fruit Gathering	31
On a Litter	33
Hassan	35
Laid up in the Hut	36
Natives Building Hut	39
Interior of House	41
Our Victims	42
Our Hostess	43
Window of the Harem	45
Old Harbor of Alexandria	47
Water Carrier,	50
Place Mohammed Ali	53
Silk Workers	56
Pompey's Pillar	59
Gathering Dates	61
Palmyra	62
Jaffa from the North	64
Pearl Merchants	67
Lydda	68
Ploughing in Palestine	69
Ramlah	71
Sidon	73
Beirut	75
Tobacco Seller	76
Flower Seller	77
Smyrna	79
Water Boy of Smyrna	81
Plain of Ephesus	83
Amphitheatre at Ephesus	84
Ruins at Ephesus	85
Pergamos	89
Ak Hissar	91
Sardis	93
Philadelphia	95
Birs Nimroud	97
Damascus	98
Public Garden	101
Street in Damascus	103
Cedar Grove	107
Temple of Baalbec	108
Fallen Pillar	109
Lake of Gennesareth	111
Magdala	112
Arab Story Teller	115
A Woman of Nazareth	117
Spring at Nazareth	119
The Carpenter's Shop	120
Valley of Shechem	122
Plain of Esdraelon	124
Nablous	127
Jacob's Well	128
Samaritan Priest	131
Evening on the Housetop	135
Temple Area and Mount of Olives	137
Street in Jerusalem	140
Pool of Hezekiah	143
Tomb of Absalom	145
Mosque of Omar	147
Church of the Holy Sepulchre	150
Stone of Unction	153
St. Stephen's Gate	156
Jerusalem and Olivet	160
Fountain of Elisha	165

LIST OF ILLUSTRATIONS.

	PAGE		PAGE
Arab at Tent Door	167	Propylon at Karnac	250
Arabs on the Plain	169	Column of Thothmes III.	251
Ruined Aqueduct near Jericho	171	Gypsy Tent	253
Banks of the Jordan	175	Temple of Ipsamboul	254
Old Khan	179	One of Them	255
Harvest-Carrying in Palestine	181	Electric Shad	256
Church of the Nativity	182	Tetrodon	256
Eastern Gleaners	183	Kanooma	257
Shepherd Boy of Bethlehem	187	Finny Pike	257
Convent of Mar Saba	189	Aboo and Selim	258
Bethlehem, looking East	192	Life in the Interior	259
Women of Bethlehem	195	Zanzibar	260
Abraham's Oak	200	Street in Tamatave	262
Hebron	201	Foliage in Madagascar	263
Cave of Adullam	202	Chief's House, Tamatave	264
Hebron and Cave of Machpelah	203	Madagascans	265
Solomon's Pool	205	Interior of Madagascar	267
Emblematic Egypt	207	Buddhist Temple	269
First Ride on a Camel	209	Ceylon Elephants	273
The Dromedary Race	211	Kandy	274
Street in Suez	212	Buddha's Tooth	275
Town of Suez	213	Temple of the Dalada	276
Street in Cairo	215	Madras Surf	277
Nilometer	217	Temple of Soubramanya	279
Mameluke's Leap	219	Rock Temple	280
Obelisk at Heliopolis	221	Milk Sellers of Madras	282
Going to Heliopolis	223	Pagoda at Pondicherry	283
Garden in Heliopolis	225	Travelling in India	285
Mary's Tree	226	Bullock Carriage	286
A Trip to the Pyramids—old style	228	Religious Mendicant	287
Foot of the Pyramid	229	Railway Travelling	291
Pyramid of Dashoor	231	Martyn's House	293
Ascent of the Pyramid	233	On the Way to the Himalayas	295
Pyramid of Sakhara	234	Benares	297
The Sphinx	239	Pavilion of Tinka	298
Funeral Procession	241	State Elephants	300
Mummy Cases	242	Indian Fakir	302
Marriage Procession	243	Panch Mahal Futtepore Sikri	304
Nile Boat	245	Jumma Mus-jid, Delhi	305
Stepped Pyramid	246	Hall of Private Audience	307
Waterwheel	247	Tomb of Rungit-sing	308
Nile Monsters	248	Golden Temple of the Sikhs	309
The Lotos	249	Floating Gardens of Srinagur	310
The Papyrus	249	Shops of Kashmir	312

RIP VAN WINKLE TRAMPING ON.

CROSSING THE RIVER.

MASTER VAN WERT was in Paris when last we parted with him, maturing his plans for a trip to the distant East. He had been reading, consulting maps, conversing with recent travellers, and gaining such information as he could, and was now looking about for some one to accompany him.

One day he was walking leisurely along the Champs Elysées, that fine promenade, striking west from Place de la Concorde one and a quarter miles, laid out with foot and carriage paths, and forming a beautiful resort for the gay and fashionable crowds, who sit and walk by hours, hearing sweet music and witnessing gay scenes. He had entered the Avenue de Neuilly, and was going toward the Triumphal

Arch, when a gentleman paused in front of him, with the exclamation,—

"Well!"

The master stopped, looked in the face of the gentleman, hesitated a moment, and then, with a smile on his face, answered,—

"Well!"

"You recognize me, then, at last?"

"Yes; though I did not expect to see you here to-day."

"Some people turn up when we least expect to see them, you know."

"Yes, and I am heartily glad to see you; it does one good to see the face of a friend in a distant land."

The gentleman was a New York merchant, who often crossed the ocean, and who was not a stranger in the streets of Paris. His name we shall call "Goodspeed."

"Let me ask," said Master Van Wert, "when you came from home, when you reached Paris, where you are staying, and where you are bound?"

"Four questions to be answered at once," said Mr. Goodspeed.

"One at a time."

"I left New York three weeks ago, and after a short stop in England came directly to Paris, where, as you see, I am; I am resting my weary self at the Grand Hotel, and next week, like a bird of passage, shall take my flight."

"Where to?"

"Where I don't want to go."

"Ah, where is that?"

"To Morocco."

"Morocco?"

"Yes, sir, against my will; but business compels me."

"I should think the trip would be an interesting and profitable one."

"It might be to one who had never been to that country. But I have been there twice, and now go for the third time."

"How do you go? By what route?"

"I proceed to Marseilles, as much of the way as I can by water, to get rid of the dust and noise of the railroad. There I shall find a steamer or sailing vessel, I do not know or care which, in which I shall go, via Malta, to Tangier, where my business lies."

"Where then?"

"Then to Algeria, Tunis, Tripoli, and Egypt. I shall merely touch at Egypt to take a steamer for Smyrna."

"A curious round-about trip."

"Yes, but one I am forced to take. And now for your plans?"

"They are not made."

"Then can I not persuade you to go with me, as I suppose you are free to go at will?"

"Is this a good season to visit Morocco?"

"As good as any. Come, pack your travelling kit, and go with me."

"I don't know. I was thinking of going to Egypt, up the Nile, into the heart of Africa."

"Perhaps you can vary your route, and take Africa later in the season. I would be glad of company, and will make my arrangements to suit yours, if you will let me have the privilege."

"I have no arrangements to make. My valise is packed, ready for a start, and I can be ready at any moment, and am inclined to go with you. I am here without much plan, except to see as much as possible in the time I have to remain."

"Let it be so fixed; and if you will tell me at what hotel you are staying, I will call upon you in the evening, and we will fix our time of starting and our mode of travel."

"All right," said the master, as he shook hands with his friend and turned away.

"This is just what I want, I think," said the master, as he moved off toward his hotel. He had seen Paris by sunlight and gaslight, at midday and at midnight. He had been to churches filled with images; to vast libraries; to cabinets of antique articles, where are objects of great curiosity and every namable and unnamable wonder; to the Bourse, where the living daily throng in such crowds; to the Invalides, where he saw the old soldiers of the Empire; to Père la Chaise, where are the tombs of Heloise and Abelard; to the Gobelins, where the curious tapestry is manufactured; to the Catacombs under the city; and to the Morgue, the resting-place of unfortunates. He had seen Paris, and was ready to go. So when Mr. Goodspeed came in that evening it was not hard to decide on plans for future work.

"I think," said the master, "that we can reach Marseilles in a way that will be more interesting to us than to go by rail all the way, which, though the most expeditious route, is the least interesting."

"How would you go?"

"By rail to Chalons, thence by steamer on the Saône to Lyons, and from Lyons, on the Rhone, to Marseilles."

"I have never been that way, and would like to enlarge my experience by pursuing that route. As I told you, I wish to escape the dust of the railroad."

"When will you be ready to start?"

"On Monday next."

"I will be ready at that time."

The friends looked over the map and saw how they were to go, and, after a quiet chat, separated, to meet at the hour for starting on their journey.

At the time appointed the two gentlemen met, and took their seats in one of the commodious second-class cars, those on French roads being much superior to those of the same grade on English roads. The master, without regret, turned his back on Paris, on that bright and beautiful day, glad to escape from the endless round of vain and frivolous amusement to the quiet scenes and cool breezes of the country. The ride from Paris to Chalons takes a long day, and lies through a country finely diversified, — now passing long rows of women toiling like slaves in the fields, now through tunnels miles in length, and anon driving across beautiful vine-covered plains. They had all kinds of company — women, with bags containing bread, meat, and wine ; jabbering Frenchmen, who kept up a conversation delightfully unintelligible ; children, who felt it a duty to cry half the way ; and a few men who used an honest tongue. They arrived at Chalons, a town of about nineteen thousand inhabitants, at eleven o'clock at night, and forthwith crowded into an omnibus, which, after an unusual amount of scolding, fretting, snapping of the whip, rolled to a dirty hotel, where they stopped for the night, and at length grumbled themselves to sleep. As soon as the sun was up, on the following day, our two travellers breakfasted, and were ready to start. They were to take steamer on the Saône, and everything gave promise of a pleasant day. And so they found it to be. The sail down the River Saône is very beautiful, and the scenery all along the banks is most delightful, though, perhaps, not equalling the castle-guarded Rhine, which every traveller wishes to see. High hills, covered with vines, cultivated to the very summit, and sloping beautifully to the river ; fine villages, sleeping on the shores ; little boats gliding up and down ; steamers now and then sweeping by, and rippling the waves to the flower-fringed bank on either side, — all render the voyage one of uninterrupted pleasure.

At the confluence of the Saône and the Rhone lies the city of Lyons, where the two gentlemen remained a day or two, when they took steamer on the Rhone for Avignon, and thence by cars to Marseilles. The ride to the latter city was a pleasant one, the cars good, and the rails smooth and easy. At Marseilles they found a little French steamer which was going to Tangier, and took passage thereon, and were soon afloat on the great sea, sailing toward the coast of Africa. On their way down they touched at Palermo, and proceeded to Malta, an interesting place to visit, and memorable as the scene of St. Paul's deliverance from shipwreck. But of this voyage the master will speak more particularly hereafter.

ST. PAUL'S BAY, MALTA.

Master Van Wert found Mr. Goodspeed a most entertaining travelling companion, a little too anxious to get along fast, having a great fund of general knowledge, and a thorough acquaintance with the various modes of travelling. He had visited the East many times, and though his tastes and pursuits were mainly in the line of business, he proved to be a very useful as well as entertaining voyager.

IN MOROCCO.

RIP VAN WINKLE TAKING A RIDE.

THE boys at home who composed the Triangle had not heard from the old master for a long time, and were beginning to be anxious about him, and impatient for another letter, when one day Charlie received a package with several foreign stamps upon it, and the familiar handwriting of Rip Van Winkle. He had been out one evening, and on his return at a late hour his father placed in his hands the letter. The clock in the distant church tower was striking, one, two, three, four, five, six, seven, eight, nine, TEN! It was time for him to go to bed, but the elastic and excited fellow could not wait until morning to show his joy, but at once started to tell Hal.

It was rather late and lonely, but he reached the house and found it dark and gloomy, the family having retired to rest. However, the lad was determined to see his friend, and so went up and pulled the bell-knob.

"Tinkle — tinkle — tinkle."

No other response, and he pulled again.

"Tinkle — tinkle — tinkle."

He waited a few minutes, and was about to ring again, when a window in an upper story was raised, and Hal put his head out to see who was at the bell.

"Who is there?"

"It's me — Charlie."

"What do you want, old fellow?"

"I have a letter from Rip Van Winkle."

"Good, first rate. When did it arrive?"

"I got it this evening, after my return from May Thornton's party."

"Have you seen Will?"

"No; but I am going over to his house."

"Well, to-morrow night we will have a meeting of the Triangle."

"Will wants it to meet at his house."

"So let it be; good night."

Charlie, in his enthusiasm, started to find Will, but concluded that his good news would keep until morning, and wisely went home, and was soon asleep in bed. The next evening the Triangle met. About thirty invited guests were present, among whom were Dr. Oldschool, Mr. Speedwell the lawyer, and Rev. Mr. Earnest, a young clergyman who had recently been settled over one of the churches, and who had been asked to come in by Hal.

"Order!" cried Charlie, bringing down his gavel precisely at the hour.

"Order!"

Order being instantly restored, Will moved that Rev. Mr. Earnest be invited to open the exercises of the evening with prayer. The motion being put and carried, Mr. Earnest prayed that the Triangle might be useful and subserve a grander purpose than was proposed at the outset; that the lads composing it might grow up to be useful men, and that Master Van Wert might be protected in his travels, and permitted to return safely to his home and friends.

"Amen," responded Dr. Oldschool.

"Amen," was the unuttered response from every heart present.

"Is there any unfinished business before the meeting?" asked the president.

No response.

"Then the letter of our travelling companion will be opened and read by Hal."

In a somewhat pretentious way Hal opened the letter, and in fine, manly tones, read the following: —

TANGIER.

DEAR BOYS,— You will doubtless be surprised at receiving a letter from Morocco, when you expected one from some part of Palestine. But "circumstances alter cases," and circumstances have led me to alter my plans very considerably, and instead of being in the Holy City I am in a city of the other extreme. This change of programme I have been led to make in consequence of having fallen in with Mr. Goodspeed, an American gentleman, who has persuaded me to come to this part of the world with him. Nor am I at all sorry, for I have time enough for my Asiatic trip after this is finished.

We took a little steamer at Marseilles for a round-about trip to this place, thinking the circuitous passage would give us good company and pleasant surroundings. But we were disappointed in all that. The vessel was a miserable one, and several times I thought we should go to the bottom, and believe we should if we had had a storm on the way. The officers were uncivil, and made their pas-

VIEW OF TANGIER.

sengers generally uncomfortable. Instead of a genteel company of civilized people we had a dirty set of vagabonds, among whom we could not recognize one decent person, with the exception of two young Americans who happened to be going to the same port that we were destined for. The crowd on board was made up mostly of the lowest class of characters, who swore and jabbered in their outlandish tongues until it seemed as if we had got into bedlam. Every part of the steamer swarmed with fleas of the most wolfish kind. We went to bed at night, but sleep was impossible. Every few minutes a hollow groan would proceed from some one of the bunks, indicative of the misery of the occupant. But you can imagine the discomfort of the passage.

On the way down we touched at one or two places, reaching Malta on the morning of the third day out. This, as you know, is the central depot of British power in the Mediterranean Sea, an island sixteen miles long, and about nine miles in the widest part, and nearly oval in shape. It is a fortified rock, bristling at every point with British cannon. The capital of the island — or rather group of islands, for under the general name come Gozo, Comino, Corminetto, and Filfla, — is Valetta, where we stopped for a few hours. The steamer anchored off the town, and we were rowed ashore by natives in small cockle-shell boats, which seemed as if they were going under water at every bend of the oars. On landing we were greeted by large numbers of Maltese sailors, women, and cats, from whom we escaped, and went up through the long narrow streets, on a tour of inspection. Everything was odd and singular; we took breakfast at a coffee-house, on very thick muddy coffee, and very coarse garlicky bread. While taking breakfast the milk gave out, and a goatherd coming along at that moment with a drove of goats and asses, the creatures were milked, and we were supplied.

We had time to visit the fortifications, the governor's palace, and the Church of St. John. In the crypts below the church, which is a

FISH MARKET.

very rich structure, are the effigies of the old knights of Malta, reposing in sculptured stone. The church has some fine specimens of painting and sculpture.

In the governor's palace were some things worth noticing,— among the rest, a gun, said to be the first made after the invention of gunpowder. It is about eight feet long, made of sheet iron, wound round with rope. What a vast change from this almost harmless thing, made since the discovery of gunpowder by Schwartz in the fourteenth century, to those murderous weapons used in the Crimea and on the banks of the Potomac!

Cotton goods and laces are considerably manufactured. The people speak a corrupt Italian, dress prettily, the men in blouses and loose trousers, and the women in neat dresses, often of their own weaving. The women are very industrious, and are found in the streets selling fish, flowers, fruits, fancy articles, and all sorts of things. The fish merchants are very different from the fish women of London, whose fame has gone all over the world for their vulgarity and abusive talk, making the name of the famous fish market of that great city — Billingsgate — synonymous with loud and insolent talk. The fish sellers of Malta are well dressed, well behaved, and often pretty girls, who drive quite a business.

The rest of the voyage to this place would have been pleasant, if the accommodations on board the steamer had not been intolerable. But the most disagreeable things come to an end, and so did the voyage, and here we are in Morocco. By consulting the map, you will see that we went quite out of our way in order to visit Malta, the steamer having some business there.

On reaching the coast opposite Tangier the question as to landing comes up, and the prospect of getting to the shore from the steamer, which is anchored a long way from the town, does not seem to be a very delightful one. But with the help of a lot of villainous-looking Arabs and negroes who came out in boats we got safely to land, and soon, in company with my friend, we were at the public house, if the miserable inn can be so designated. But we found several Europeans there, and in their company things began to look a little more inviting and comfortable.

My friend at once made arrangements to attend to his business matters, while I connected myself with some Germans who were travelling for pleasure. On going out into the streets we found them narrow, tortuous, filthy, and full of stolid-looking people, many of whom were armed to the teeth, and looked like brigands and assassins. The inhabitants of Tangier dress in loose robes, most of them —the robes, not the people—having been white once, but now sadly soiled; once probably whole, but now sadly tattered and torn.

There is a square, intersected by the principal street of the place which makes a kind of centre, and the business of the place, the excitement, and general interest, cluster about it.

At night the streets are dark, not a light being seen in any direction, and when you are out late you will stumble over the bodies of the white or dirt-colored Arabs who have gone to sleep against the sides of the houses by the way. Do the best you might and you could not help tumbling over the inanimate creatures, who as you trampled on them only gave an expressive grunt.

The Moors and Jews are numerous, and all the tongues of the earth seem to be jabbered by the people who about midday are found in the square. The Jews are largely engaged in trading, and, as elsewhere, they are extensively engaged in banking operations. The Jewesses of Morocco have a great reputation for personal beauty. Describing that beauty one extravagant writer says, "It is an opulent and splendid beauty, with large black eyes, broad low forehead, full red lips, and statuesque form—a theatrical beauty, that looks well from a distance, and produces applause rather than sighs in the beholder." We went through the Jewish quarter, into some of the Hebrew houses, and saw many Jewish ladies, but noticed nothing that came up to this idea of admiration. I think the notion of beauty in the Jewish women of this empire is derived from the pleasant contrast they form with the mulatto women, who are seen in their untidy robes and filthy dresses.

SERPENT CHARMERS.

At first I felt unsafe, but in a few days I became convinced that there was no reason to fear ill treatment or personal violence. A European seems to be considered a sort of public guest, to be treated with respect, and protected, rather than ill used. When a mulatto is found guilty of abusing any one he is mounted upon a donkey, and being securely tied thereon is whipped through the public streets until the blood pours from his lacerated body.

On a hill overlooking the place is the *casba*, the fortification that commands the town. It does not seem, to a person accustomed to European fortifications, to be a very formidable seat of military operations. But as a place to obtain a fine view of the white roofs and glittering tops of the public buildings, with a vast extent of country around, it is well worth a visit. It looks as though a war vessel in the harbor would soon batter it down, if heavy guns could be brought to play upon it.

The natives find much pleasure in the ride or walk along the fine beach to Cape Malabet, and on a fine day the whole way may be seen crowded with all sorts of people, in all sorts of costumes, jabbering in all sorts of languages. What Central Park is to New Yorkers, this long drive on the Malabet beach is to the people here. The fête days are numerous, and when one of these occurs the sight witnessed is novel in the extreme. The "Antique and Horrible" processions, which take place in some of the New England cities on the morning of Independence Day, are far outdone by the crowds of negroes, mulattoes and Arabs that fill the streets, with rude instruments of music, showy banners, and grotesque masquerading. The great day is the fête of Mahomet.

The public dancers are numerous, and as far as I could judge well patronized. All the sports of Morocco are very solemnly conducted. The music on all occasions is dirge-like, the dancing is solemn, and all the fun and mirth is acted out without a smile, as if it was part of a funeral service. The fact is, the people are too lazy to smile; if they try, the effort seems to overcome them. An air of indescribable indolence is on everything and everybody.

After we had been at Tangier a few days, the Germans, of whom I have spoken, organized a company to go to other parts of the empire. They invited me to go with them, and Mr. Goodspeed having business on his hands, and not being able to give me his attention, I was glad to accept. A government escort was provided us, and one morning we drove out of Tangier, mounted on the most sorry-looking set of horses that were ever brought into one lot. Some were lean and lank; others were minus mane and tail; others were scrubby little things that looked as if they would break down under the weight

THE INTERIOR.

of a full-grown man. But they had the merit of speed. Bad as they looked, "the go" was in them, and when we capered, cantered, trotted, raced out of Tangier, a hooting, yelling crowd of boys and men ran along with us, bidding us a kindly though boisterous adieu.

Well, Fez—what of Fez? Our caravan, which had become quite a formidable company, went into Fez just at night, after a journey of thrilling adventures and exciting incidents. When we came within sight of the walls of the city, we received a friendly greeting. It seemed as if the whole place had turned out to welcome us, and we entered in the midst of the most unintelligible tumult. The view of Fez from a distance is very fine. The walls are seen to great advantage, and above them the towers, monuments, and tall trees rise in striking beauty. But on entering the gates, the city appears dilapidated and broken to pieces, and an air of desolation is over everything. Once elegant Moorish palaces are in a sad state of decay.

The public buildings are poor, though there are some worthy of inspection. The mosques of El-Cavuin and Muley-Edrio are imposing externally, and said to be gorgeous internally, though we were not allowed to enter there. The Hebrew synagogue is also a prominent building, situated in the Jews' quarter, for in every great city the Hebrews, that wonderful people, find lodgment. The bazaars and shops are similar to those in other African cities. The merchant sits surrounded with his wares, looking as if he did not care whether he sold or not. But to a stranger these shops in the narrow streets are very attractive, and the grotesqueness of the arrangements only enhances the interest.

There is at Fez a University,—House of Science, as it is called, and the city was in former days quite an important seat of learning. The Emperor of Morocco has three residences, and this is one of them, and he spends about one-third of his time here. When he is in the city the whole place is full of interest. Trade revives, and the people of surrounding sections come in to see the court parades and military processions.

The manufacture of morocco, the red leather which has become so famous, and which takes its name from the country, is carried on to a great extent here, and a large number of persons are engaged in it. Jewelry, saddlery, red woollen caps, and some other manufactures are carried on, but to no great extent. How the people get

MODE OF TRANSPORTATION.

a living it is hard to tell. However, the cost of living is very small. What would be expended by a New York clerk on his dinner would support a dozen of the Berbers or negroes of this place a whole week.

The Wad-el-Jubor—River of Pearls—runs through the city, dividing it into old and new, but the whole looks old enough to have survived the flood. The city is about eighty miles from Tangier. Between the two places are several towns, not worth stopping at by one who has not unlimited time at his command.

MOROCCO.

Our caravan—which has become a small army of cooks, porters, guides, grooms, and all sorts of servant travellers—started from Fez on one sultry morning, and slowly moved toward the capital of the empire, and after several nights of camping and several days of riding saw the walls of the city standing on the plain. These walls are six miles in circumference. They are built of lime and earth, ground into a cement. There are square towers rising, one hundred and fifty feet apart. There are eleven gates piercing these walls, and at most of them crowds are going out and coming in all the time. Morocco is not a brilliant capital of an empire. The houses are generally of one story, with flat roofs. The streets are narrow and dark, and one shudders to go through them after sundown. Things look a little better when you get into the houses. The apartments generally surround a court, in the centre of which is a fountain or some piece of statuary. The rooms are finished elaborately, and but for the dilapidated state of everything, some of them would have the appearance of elegance. Rich carvings are found in many of the houses, showing a style of finish which belonged to earlier and better days.

The emperor's palace is outside the walls, and the grounds are very extensive, and are kept in very good order. While not comparable with many of the royal gardens of Europe, they are quite beautiful. To some parts of the extensive grounds travellers are admitted, and Europeans receive as much attention from the officials as if they were distinguished citizens. When disgusted with the confusion, heat, and indistinguishable smells of the city, it was a real luxury to get outside the walls and revel in the purity and sweetness of the royal gardens. It is also the best place to see the royal family and officers of state, and distinguished guests who are in attendance on the court. The palace itself is not remarkable, and many a hotel at home would far surpass it in splendor. You are tired, doubtless, of hearing about mosques and public buildings, and these I will say nothing about.

COSTUMES IN MOROCCO.

The population is what you would naturally expect from a conglomeration of people of all colors mingled together in uneducated and unrefined masses, where the brute life often appears to prevail over the human.

MOGADORE.

After seeing Morocco, our caravan started again, and travelled one hundred and twenty miles, and reached Mogadore after six days. Turn to your maps, boys. The town is on the Atlantic sea-coast, and to reach it we have travelled through some of the wildest and roughest scenes in the empire of Morocco. It is one of the most important seaports in the country, though the population is scarcely twenty thousand. Ostrich feathers, gum, hides, almonds, wool, and several other articles are shipped from here in great abundance. The place has suffered much from the fortunes of war. The French took it in 1844, and the marks of the severe bombardment are still seen.

On our way here we had a fine opportunity to see the people in the villages, and the field hands getting in the produce of the earth, the half-clad negroes carrying on their heads or shoulders burdens that might weary a horse.

At this place I shall part with the Germans who have composed the caravan. They will push southward along the coast, while I shall sail for Tangier to meet Mr. Goodspeed. I shall not be sorry to be out of Morocco, though the other countries I have to visit may not furnish any better entertainment. Since we have been here we had wild experiences, of which I will speak to you after my return. Mogadore will hold me only long enough to find a vessel to take me out. There is less of the negro element than in Morocco, though the blacks are well represented. The population is mainly divided into Moors and Jews. These two classes inhabit different sections of the town. The citadel part is occupied by the former, and the lower part by the latter. Population divides itself in nearly the same way in all the towns and cities that we have seen. The Jews attend to the banking, the Moors to the manufacturing, and the negroes to the drudgery. The negro is used for almost everything that requires hard labor, even to lugging passengers on their shoulders across the little rivers, and one or two rides of that kind I have had. On one occasion

FRUIT GATHERERS AT RIO.

while I was out hunting with a negro guide, the tide came in, and as usual at high water, surrounded Mogadore, the town being on a plateau, surrounded with marshes. The only way for me to get back was to wade, and my black guide taking me on his shoulders, put me through, as nicely as a horse could have done. It was a curious kind of riding, and the animal seemed to enjoy the sport as much as his rider. Once or twice, when he came near dumping me into water, he indulged in an immoderate laugh of satisfaction.

RIP VAN WINKLE.

IN ALGERIA.

ON A LITTER.

RIP VAN WINKLE remained at Mogadore some time longer than he expected to have done, on account of circumstances which he will detail in his next letter, and when he set sail he was devoutly grateful to the kind providence which had enabled him to obtain a glimpse of the empire of Morocco and get out safely in spite of experiences with bandits, with an unhealthy climate, with jungle adventures, and all the annoyances one meets in a country which is separated from the arts and culture of Europe, only by a narrow strait, which is easily crossed, but which, as far as the civilization of Morocco is concerned, might as well be as deep and as wide as the Atlantic Ocean.

ALGIERS.

From a boy the name of Algiers has been a terror to me. In my early days it was associated in my mind with atrocious piracies that made the world shudder. Previous to 1815, when Commodore Decatur destroyed an Algerine fleet, and, sailing into this harbor, forced the dey to surrender all American prisoners found in his dungeons, Algiers was noted for the extent of its piratical operations. Then, in 1816, England took it up, and a British fleet, under Lord Exmouth, bombarded the city. Then the French sent a fleet to do mischief, and that great power arrayed itself against the piracy of the Algerines, which had become so notorious that the name of Algiers was hated throughout the commercial world. But Algerine piracy has been suppressed. The sea is no longer molested by the clipper ships, bearing the black flag or the skull and cross-bones, and Algiers is so thoroughly under French control, that life is nearly as safe as in Paris.

Before speaking of this city and country, I will tell you how I got away from Mogadore. The German caravan left me at the inn, and at once I set about finding a vessel bound for Tangier. But no one offering itself, I determined to have a few days of sport in the interior. It was somewhat hazardous, but selecting a fine, comely black, named Hassan, I started out one morning, to be gone two or three days. The shooting was good, and the game plenty, and everything went well until the second day, when at noon, while taking our dinner, Hassan leaped wildly to his feet, exclaiming, "Lion! lion!" and betook himself to the nearest tree. I did the same thing, and soon both of us felt ashamed of our flight, for nothing appeared but a wild boar, who went tramping along at a tearing rate. Seeing what it was, and anxious to get a shot at the animal, I leaped from the tree, and in my descent fell somewhat unfortunately, and sprained my ankle, and it caused me great pain. Hassan got me to the hut of a native, which was not far away, but by the time I reached the hut the ankle was badly swollen, and the kind and faithful fellow, with the assistance of the proprietor of the hut, was obliged to cut away my boot and apply cooling lotions to the inflammation; but in spite of all they could do, and my own determination, I was obliged to go to bed and stay there two or three days. The negro who owned the hut gave me up the only bed he had, which was a clean one, overhung by a sort of rude canopy of his own manufacture. The hut contained little beside the bed and a chest, and the only occupant until our arrival was the negro, who kept a pet goat, that had free access to the hut, and who as soon as it saw me on its master's bed became my constant attendant, refusing to leave me for an hour. It was a noble creature, seeming to have the instincts of a human being. It hung around me, sprang upon the bed, lapped my hands, and seemed to manifest a reasoning fondness.

HASSAN.

Wishing to get to town as soon as possible, Hassan formed a litter, and securing a couple of negroes, I was borne back, while the guide kept by my side, through the swamps and bushes, where the way was almost impassable.

Soon after, I found a coasting vessel bound for Tangier, and took passage. We stopped a few hours at each of several little seaport towns, for which I was glad, as it gave me an opportunity to go ashore and see more of the country. At Asamar, Rabuat, Mehedia, and other places, we put in, but soon put out again, and in due time arrived at Tangier, where I found Mr. Goodspeed, and he being ready to start, we shipped at once for this port, where we now are.

LAID UP IN THE HUT.

Algiers is finely situated on the bay, and the buildings form an amphitheatre. It is a walled city, and is the capital of the country, Being the headquarters of French power in Algiers, the European population is large, and there is a "Frenchiness" not seen anywhere else in the country. The hotels are fair, the mosques elegant, the government houses, bank, and cathedral respectable buildings. There are several colleges, a bishop's house, and the usual accompaniments of such a city. There is much of the appearance of a European city Steamers ply from this to several other ports, and the constant coming and going of vessels makes the place very lively.

Mr. Goodspeed having finished his business here, we discussed the propriety of going further into the country. One day we approached our landlord, a Frenchman, who had long lived here, and my friend said to him, —

"Would it be worth our while to visit Constantia?"

"Constantia?"

"Yes."

"What you want to know about Constantia?"

"Whether it would be wise for us to go there?"

"*Oui.*"

"That is, would we see enough to pay us for so long a journey?"

"*Oui.* Constantia is a much fine city. I know all about him."

"How large a place?"

"Very large," stretching his arms apart.

"But how many inhabitants?"

"Inhabitants?"

"Yes; how many people?"

"*Oui*, ze peoples much; thirty thousand of him."

"Had we better go there?"

"No go, bad place; bad peoples in the woods — very far off."

"How far?"

"One hundred miles you call him, and fifty, sixty, seventy, eighty more."

"One hundred and eighty miles?"

"*Oui.*"

"How about Bona?"

"No good! No good!"

"Or Oran?"

"You no go to any place. You stay here; you be safe. When you want to go, you go to the ship. No go to ze peoples."

And on many accounts we concluded that it was not safe to venture into the country. First, there is little to see. There is a remarkable sameness in all the negro villages, and the inland cities and towns are devoid of special interest. Then it is not quite safe to be about among the inhabitants of the interior. The quarrels among themselves, the jealousy of strangers, and the general character of the people, makes travelling anywhere but in the most public places somewhat hazardous. On these accounts we concluded to make a hasty visit, and take an early departure.

RIP VAN WINKLE.

IN TUNIS AND TRIPOLI.

NATIVES BUILDING A HUT.

ONE morning a steamer landed a dozen passengers in the harbor of Tunis, the capital of the Regency of the same name, and among them were Rip Van Winkle and Mr. Goodspeed, both of whom had had quite enough of the Algerines. How they fared in Tunis will be told by the Master.

TUNIS.

After a wakeful night we landed in the chief city of Tunis, glad to get out of the steamer which took us from Algiers. I think, boys, you will not blame me for not getting reconciled to some of the annoyances we meet on the little steamboats that ply along the northern coast of Africa. They generally run in the night, and stop and load or unload by day. To sleep is impossible, for we have strange bed-fellows. They are such as Dean Swift alludes to in a stanza of his,—

> "So, naturalists observe, a flea
> Has smaller fleas that on him prey;
> And these have smaller still to bite 'em;
> And so proceed *ad infinitum.*"

Jonathan must have been a passenger on one of these boats at some time. As we approached the city, it presented a very fine appearance, and looked as if a great deal of comfort might be found in it. But it has the narrow streets, the low rude houses, the squalid poverty, the filthy habits, and the treacherous manners of Algiers.

The city, which has nearly two hundred thousand inhabitants, is surrounded by a double wall, and defended by a strong fortification. There are a plenty of mosques, a Moorish college, one or two theatres, some public baths, with manufactories of cotton, linen, and woollen goods. The place has great antiquity, and has had a singular history. Like Carthage, whose ancient site is not far off, it traces its record back to a very remote period.

Perhaps, boys, you imagine that I am in a country of sultry heat, but in this you are mistaken. The temperature of Tunis in winter averages 55° and in summer only 85°, while the mean of the year is 70°. So you see the people of the sea coast have a delightful climate. But when you go into the interior, and approach the great desert which begins within a short distance of the sea, you find the heat more intense.

While at Tunis we went out on two or three occasions to hunt. Before we started, the residents told us that we should find plenty of lions, wild horses, panthers, and wolves to shoot. To tell the truth we did not care much to see the panthers and lions, and did not. If there were any of these inhabitants of the forests they did not trouble us. We got upon the track of two or three wolves, but our inexperience in hunting allowed them to get out of our way. So I shall not be able to bring home a stuffed lion, as a present to the Triangle. We did, however, do some deer and antelope shooting, and took back with us some specimens which would have made a show in Washington market if they could have been hung there, with the inscription, "Shot in Tunis, by Rip Van Winkle."

The old Roman ruins we did not feel it safe to visit. The barbarous people murder and rob any unprotected stranger that comes to see their country, and unless a large guard is obtained, no one knows, when he leaves Tunis, how he will get back. Though we did not go far away, we had some rough adventures, and one night, while stopping in a hut in the woods, were surrounded by the wild Arabs, and should have been robbed if not killed,

INTERIOR OF HOUSE.

had we not made a vigorous demonstration with our firearms, by which the barbarians were frightened away, supposing we were more numerous and better armed than we were.

OUR VICTIMS.

TRIPOLI.

Coming along the coast we reached this city, the capital of the province of the same name. Like Algiers, Tripoli has been famous in ages past for its piracy. One of its governors, Dragut, somewhere about the year 1550, was a noted corsair, and, under his rule, the State became the headquarters of the worst class of men who ever sailed upon the ocean. The ships of no nation were safe. The commerce of all nations was at the mercy of these lawless depredators, who became so bold and defiant that they were hated in every civilized land. This state of things lasted from the time of Dragut to the year 1816, when the British compelled the Tripolitans to abandon their infamous practices upon the high seas. Thanks to war steamers, pirates have little chance in our times.

The city of Tripoli is an uninteresting place. The houses are low, generally of one story, with flat roofs. The streets are narrow and filthy, the inhabitants boisterous and treacherous, and the customs and

A LADY OF CEYLON.

manners of the foreign merchants are little calculated to make the place attractive.

The caravansary at which we are stopping, though small, is neatly kept. The head of the house is a woman of fine appearance. Only once have we seen her. Her servants are mostly men, but she rules them well. She is an illustration of the value of brains. On one occasion one of the table waiters became insolent, and refused to fill our orders or answer our calls. We appealed to the head of the house, expecting to see a man, to whom we could state our grievance, but we were indeed surprised to find ourselves confronted by an elegantly dressed lady, who conversed fluently in English and who received us with as much dignity as could the Queen of England. On stating our case, her eyes flashed, her hands were brought impressively together, and the offender was sent for. On his appearance she showered upon him a torrent of angry words, under which the fellow, whom now we began to pity, stood cowering with shame and fright. Assuring us that the offence should not be repeated she dismissed us, and ordered the fellow to the stables, where he was kept in disgrace until after we left. He did not appear in the dining-room during our stay in the place. We made several excursions out into the country, when it was safe and pleasant to go, and saw something of the rural districts, impressed every moment with the immense failure of European civilization to penetrate into Africa. The moment we left the seaport towns all traces of European institutions vanished, and we were thrown back into the blackness of barbarism.

RIP VAN WINKLE.

IN ALEXANDRIA.

WINDOW OF THE HAREM.

In a steamer running from Tripoli to Alexandria, Rip Van Winkle and his fellow-traveller took passage, and early one morning reached the latter port, where they were to spend a few days and then part company. The merchant was to return to Europe, while the master was not quite decided which way to go. He had plenty of time on his hands, was not pushed for funds, and could take things as he pleased, and he was prepared to go in such directions as would give him the best facilities for seeing the world and acquiring information.

ALEXANDRIA.

The Triangle will be glad to learn that I have got through with the Arabs, Bedouins, and negroes of Morocco, Algiers, and Tripoli, with no damage to my physical proportions. I have been in some tight places, but can honestly say that I never had "hair-breadth 'scapes." In coming to countries of more interest to you, I shall be more specific in my details, and more full in my description, for I remember how carefully you charged me to tell you all about Egypt, when I should reach that country. Well, I am here; and though I do not propose to remain long at the present time, I will give you all the particulars I can think of, or rather all that the limits of a letter will allow me to write about. While you are wearing furs and mufflers, and getting your sport in coasting, skating, sleighing, and frolicking in your youth among the frozen streams, falling snow, and drifting ice of New York, I am here in the intense heat of the dusty plains and arid deserts of Egypt.

On approaching the coast you are conscious of a stifling heat, as from a furnace. In my own case, I awoke one morning, after a fearful voyage, and found the steamer lying still outside the harbor, and on going on deck, experienced sensations very much like that of a man who had put his head into a heated oven. The spars, rigging, and deck of the steamer were covered with a fine red dust from the desert, which had met us twenty miles away, and clung obstinately to every object on which it rested. The pilot who took us in was a native, and looked much better fitted for the arena of a circus, or the stage of a theatre, than for the wheel-house of a steamer. He had on loose, flowing trousers, a close-fitting red jacket, with black and gold braid ornamentation, while on his curly head rested a little jaunty cap, the whole forming an attire so novel and grotesque, that the stranger, up to that moment unfamiliar with the costumes of the country, was in doubt whether a man or woman had taken possession of the ship. Nimble as a cat, he ran about the vessel, chattering like a black-

OLD HARBOR OF ALEXANDRIA.

bird, in an unknown tongue, until, safely through the narrow passages and dangerous straits, he brought the steamer to her anchorage in front of the city.

No sooner was the cable out than a hundred jabbering Arabs sprung on board from light feluccas, in which they had come out from land. It seemed for a time as if we had got into Bedlam. These invaders all talked at once in their strange accents, gesticulated to each other and to us, and everything was in confusion. Some were custom-house officers, some hotel proprietors, some mail agents, some were beggars, some were thieves, and a few were Alexandrian gentlemen and merchants who had come out to meet friends. The custom-house officers were overhauling our luggage. The hotel proprietors, with cards in hand, were recommending in unknown tongue their various public inns. The mail agents were pointing out their mail-bags. The beggars were following us about like spaniels, whining "backsheesh! backsheesh!" The thieves were on the alert to steal anything, from a silk handkerchief to a gold watch. Merchants, thieves, beggars, all looked alike in their red caps, loose garments, untrimmed beards, and unwashed faces.

And there before us was Alexandria, with its domes, minarets, mosques and palaces, sitting like a queen on the shores of the great sea.

The city of Alexandria, you know, is situated on the mouth of the Nile, and occupies a large place in history. In ancient times it vied with Rome in military greatness; with Athens in literature, and with Tyre in commercial importance. Early in the history of the Church, Christianity was planted there by St. Mark, who organized the first congregation. Philosophy and science there found numerous and influential patrons, and the great library founded by Ptolemy Soter 290 B.C. which numbered 500,000 volumes in an age when books were comparatively few, made Alexandria a place of great literary renown. From the time the city was founded by Alexander the Great 332 B.C.

for twelve centuries it was a place of immense wealth and extensive commerce, the great centre to which the trade of Europe and the Mediterranean with Persia and the distant East converged. But Time levelled its walls and War slaughtered its inhabitants. It incurred the hostility of Rome, its military rival, and was again and again sacked by Caracalla, Aurelian and Diocletian. Its commerce drifted to other ports; its wealth aided to build up Constantinople; its power faded before superior races, and its ancient glory went to sad decay. The great temple of Serapis was destroyed by the Patriarch Theophilus, who left no vestige of its former splendor. The famous library was used by Caliph Omar to light the fires of his four hundred royal baths, the Saracen declaring, "If these Grecian books agree with the Koran they are useless, if not they should be destroyed." The population which once rivalled the London of to-day dwindled to a handful of wandering vagabonds.

Mahomet Ali endeavored to avert the ruin, and, by the revival of trade, the promotion of commerce, and the rebuilding of the port, made modern Alexandria a place of considerable activity. The present city has sixty thousand inhabitants, made up of all the nations of the earth.

The first thing a traveller meets on landing in Alexandria, or in any other Egyptian city, is some adventure with the donkey-boys, a queer set of beings whose curious antics and strange gibberish lead us to query whether they belong to the monkey tribe or are real, thorough specimens of the *genus homo*. I had heard of them, and knew nearly what to expect, for all travellers have had about the same experience with them. As we set our feet on shore, we were attacked by almost a hundred of them in one solid rabble. They had been waiting the arrival of the steamer, ready for a cargo of new victims. They came on like hungry wolves, shouting in all sorts of dialects, seizing our baggage, pulling our clothing, crowding us in one direction and pushing us in another, one urging us to ride his donkey for this reason, and another for that; and one or two of our party who were men of small stature and light weight were actually lifted from their feet and mounted on the little frowzy animals, before they knew what the boys were doing with them.

EASTERN WATER SELLER.

While in the midst of this hubbub, which was as unintelligible to us as a scene among the hackmen in a New York depot would be to a company of newly-landed Chinese, we espied, at a little distance, a vehicle, half way between an old-fashioned baggage-wagon and a modern hearse, and without knowing, indeed hardly caring whether it went to the hotel or the graveyard, we sprang for it, hoping we should escape the annoyance. But we had a practical application of the old adage, "Out of the frying-pan into the fire," for, though the donkey drivers fell back, a hungry pack of dragomen, or professional guides, followed us, offering their services and stating their terms. They were ludicrously, alarmingly persistent. They filled the hearse until the crazy vehicle cracked and groaned beneath the burden. They climbed upon the outside and yelled over our shoulders. They gesticulated, screamed, howled, and made the whole way hideous. Each one had a bag of greasy recommendations given him by English or American travellers whom he had taken up the Nile, or piloted through Syria. Some of these papers denounced the bearers as worthless vagabonds, heartless liars, persistent cheats, and arrant knaves, but the fellows not being able to read had no idea of the impression made on us, as each one handed us his worn and soiled document, saying in triumph — "Judge of my character."

The omnibus fortunately took us to a fine hotel, conducted on European principles, where a traveller could be as well accommodated as in London or Paris. This hotel was situated on the grand square of Alexandria, and from its balconies in front fine views were obtained in all directions. On looking out of the windows, or from the porticos, the square is found, like our parks at home, to be filled with people. But, unlike our parks, the people are made up of all nationalities, and there appears a vast variety of costumes and colors, the Greek and the Turk, the Nubian and the Bedouin, the Frenchman from Paris, and the Arab from the desert, the Englishman from the banks of the Thames, and the Abyssinian from the upper Nile! Each has his own peculiar costume. The Egyptians are clad mostly in the flowing Oriental garb, varying from a mere white cloth around the body, leaving the major part of the person exposed, to the full Turkish or Egyptian suit, with its gay colors and fantastic decorations.

Around the square of Alexandria, which to the natives is what the Common is to Boston, are the consulates of the various nations, and waving over them are the distinctive flags, showing where the accredited representive of each foreign government can be found. There were the tricolors of France flapping lazily in the sun, representing yesterday a kingdom, to-day a republic, to-morrow an empire. There was the Union Jack, the royal ensign of Great Britain, on whose proud possessions the sun never goes down. There was the crimson Crescent of Turkey, symbol of the waning Ottoman. And there, too, were the Stars and Stripes.

I shall never forget the emotions with which I looked on that beautiful flag, which so recently in our own country was in peril. It is worth a voyage to Europe, to feel as every patriot must feel when looking up to this standard of our country, waving in a foreign sky — the "Stars and Stripes," suggested as our national symbol by John Adams, adopted by Congress in 1777, and first in battle at the surrender of Burgoyne, and borne out upon the ocean by Paul Jones, from whose mast-head it first fluttered in a European port. At home we look upon it as a piece of holiday bunting, but waving in a foreign land, flapping against the thrones of kings, it is the emblem of self-government, constitutional liberty, and Democratic ideas and purposes, — the symbol of universal freedom and political equality.

Beside the peculiarity of costume, and the adventures among the donkey boys, the traveller in Egypt is struck with several things which are so novel as to draw his attention, challenge his criticism, and provoke his mirth.

The means of locomotion is one thing. There are few horses, fewer carriages, but innumerable donkeys. Little children, sometimes five or six of them on one beast, are seen; women with their faces covered, looking like ghosts, sitting on their knees in a most awkward way, go trotting along; fat portly men of aldermanic size amble through the streets looking as if they would break the legs of the little creatures, nothing of which can be discerned under the flowing robes of the rider but the ears and heels; now and then two boys appear, sitting back to back, one grasping the mane, the other clinging to what, in days gone by, used to be the tail of the creature, that seems to enjoy the fun as much as they do. The whole spectacle is so novel to an American, who is accustomed to ponderous street cars, heavy omnibuses, and stately vehicles, that his face is

PLACE MOHAMMED ALI.

constantly covered with a broad laugh. The ludicrousness of the whole thing would soon cure the most confirmed dyspeptic.

Then one is struck with the blindness which prevails extensively. About one-third of the people seem to have some trouble with their eyes. It is distressing to see so much of this disease. Blind children, blind men, blind women, and even blind mules and donkeys, are met in all directions. The cause of this blindness is found mainly in the filthy, wretched habits of the people. The children are actually covered, and literally eaten up, with flies. It is not uncommon for a mother to carry her babe through the streets covered with these insects, without trying to brush them off.

Somehow the Egyptian fly has swifter motion, and a sharper sting than any other. However it may have been with the other plagues which were sent upon this hapless land in the days of Moses, the plague of flies still continues. To a stranger the insect is exceedingly troublesome, while the natives seem to consider it one of the luxuries of the climate. The question is sometimes asked, What God made mosquitoes for? A man on the banks of the Nile asks with double emphasis, What the Egyptian fly was made for.

It generally aims at the eye, strikes in at once, boring like a gimlet into the sufferer's flesh, and as you lift your hand to brush it off, you find its poisonous weapon so deeply embedded, that you kill the insect in dislodging it. The infection is carried from eyes that are diseased to those that are not, and thus they keep up a perpetual system of inoculation.

Some say that a superstition among the people, that the fly is a sacred insect, prevents its destruction. Others say that mothers extinguish the right eye of the male child, that he may not be forced into the army. But doubtless the real cause of the prevalent blindness is the utter filthiness of the children, and the inattention to personal cleanliness among adults. Dr. Smith, formerly mayor of Boston, who looked at the phenomenon as a medical man, thinks that in addition to the uncleanliness of the people, the visual inability may come from wearing the turban and the tarboosh, there being no rim or visor to shade the eyes from the sun which, pouring on the heated sand, reflects the light with all the intensity of a mirror.

Dr. Smith states — you may believe it or not — that an English lady told him that an opinion prevails in Egypt, that it is exceedingly disastrous to wash an infant until it is quite a year old, consequently from the hour they are born into the world, to the termination of twelve months — I quote his language — "the dirty brats are never washed." Whether this is true or not I cannot tell from actual observation, but of course it must be, coming from a lady; and certainly, I have seen children who looked as if they had not been washed for a dozen years, and who would take all the waters of the Nile to make them clean.

But whatever may be the cause of the blindness, it is fearfully prevalent. Blind men stand in the streets, asking your charity on every corner; men blind of an eye look out at you from the little window of the shop where nicknacks and gimcracks are sold; the donkey boy, whose half blind beast you hire, is blind of an eye; his mother, who comes to help him out of the scrape into which you are sure to get with him when you settle for his services, is blind of an eye; his father, who comes to help his mother, is blind of an eye; the waiter at the hotel unfortunately has some trouble with his eyes; the landlord is obliged to shut one eye and squint dreadfully before he answers the honest question you ask him; and before you have been in Egypt a week, you find yourself asking your friends if there is not something the matter with your own eyes.

The first night in Egypt is a trying one. To say nothing of the fleas, which are monstrous in size and ferocious in disposition, the dogs and donkeys manage to prevent sleep. The dogs of Alexandria are very numerous, and go at large, a ferocious, half-starved race of creatures, looking more like wolves and jackals

SILK WINDERS.

than common dogs. They run in droves, and prey upon the flesh of horses and donkeys, or, perchance, upon some human being who falls dead or drunken in the street. At night, these savage creatures keep up a terrific howling and barking. One solitary dog will commence, and in a moment he will be joined by another, then another, until it seems as if forty thousand dogs were uniting in one prolonged canine chorus. At first you are amazed; then amused; then, as the howls come in, just like the parts in some modern fashionable church music, — tenor, soprano, contralto, bass, — each chasing the other through rhyme and measure, you are obliged to break out into a hearty laugh at the grotesque ideas which are suggested.

The donkeys also make the night hideous. Almost every man, boy, and woman in Egypt keeps a donkey. The animal is sometimes tied in the street; sometimes left in the front entry with the door open; sometimes put into the spare room of the house; and sometimes taken to bed with the owner, or rather the owner goes to bed with the donkey! You have just got asleep by dint of hard work, — stuffing the pillows in your ears to keep out the barking of the dogs, and counting a hundred backwards, to make you forget that a half million fleas have gone to bed with you, — when you start up, every sense awake, wondering what that noise could be, — thunder, earthquake, or the hotel tumbling down. First one unearthly noise from one brutish throat, then another, and another, ten, twenty, a hundred of them, all in one deafening bray.

While everything in Alexandria is novel and interesting, there are few special objects and these are soon seen. Pompey's Pillar outside the city, standing alone in its solitary pomp, ninety-nine feet high and thirty feet in circumference, is a real wonder. Of its origin, how it came here, with what instruments it was quarried, by what process it was raised to its present elevation, but little is known. An inscription, deciphered by Wilkinson, showing that it was erected by Publius, prefect of Egypt in honor of Diocletian, whose name it should bear instead of that of Pompey, is all the information that has come down to us. It is a striking object, a wonderful comment on the skill of the ancients, proving that they must have had machinery which has been lost for nearly forty centuries.

The shaft of the pillar, between the base and the elegantly wrought capital is seventy-three feet high, of polished red granite. A woman, looking as I have always supposed the "Witch of Endor" looked, was guarding it when I was there, to prevent any mutilations, for unless such things were guarded they would be chipped to pieces and carried away by the vandal hordes from Europe and America, whose antiquarian tastes are limited to the mutilation of works of art, and whose sacrilegious hands are used in despoiling the most venerable relics of antiquity.

Cleopatra's Needles are two obelisks, one of which fell down, and was long almost entirely embedded in the earth, whence it was removed to New York and now stands in Central Park. Though named for the wicked daughter of Ptolemy Auletes, they were erected long before her times. The other obelisk has been removed to London, and stands on the banks of the Thames. It is seventy feet high, and covered with curious hieroglyphics that prove that it was brought to Alexandria from the ancient temple of the sun at Heliopolis, and like Pompey's Pillar shows the grandeur of the ancient structures, and the skill of those by whom these shafts were quarried and set up.

These few relics of the former glory of Alexandria are all that remain, and much of the present city is as tasteless and modern as are the new-fangled buildings in the mushroom cities of our Western States.

Doubtless all these obelisks were once in the "Temple of the Sun.' Whatever may have been their history since, or the names they now bear, they were once parts of the templed city, which was the centre and glory of Egyptian worship.

The traveller also finds some ancient catacombs, but the mum-

POMPEY'S PILLAR.

mies have been removed — used for fuel or converted into an agent for fertilization — the decorations destroyed, and the passages filled with filth and rubbish. The memory of the dead has been lost in the dust of ages; the generations, as they have marched by, have trampled down into utter oblivion even the names of those who once reposed in these elegant receptacles of death.

The funeral customs of the Egyptians are very peculiar. Almost every morning we were awakened by the wailing mourners as they carried the corpse to the grave. When a person is about to die, in Egypt, they place him with his face toward Mecca, and let him expire looking toward the tomb of the Moslem prophet. When life is extinct they wrap the body in a shroud of cloth, — cotton if the man is poor, and silk if he is rich. White and green are the colors generally used; blue is expressly interdicted. A poor child is often carried to the grave in a box or tray on the head of a woman. A rich man's funeral procession will often have with it two or three camels loaded with simple articles of food, to be distributed among the spectators at the grave.

I was awakened on the Sabbath morning after my arrival by a strange outcry in the street, and on looking out saw one of these unique funeral processions. First came about fifty men and boys with tin horns, rude drums, and unearthly sounding gongs, making a most hideous outcry. Next came a dozen venerable-looking men — priests, I suppose — repeating solemnly, "There is no god but God, and Mohammed is his prophet." Then followed a number of persons bearing the body on a bier. The corpse was draped in gay and showy colors, and the dashing turban of the deceased lay on the outside. Immediately behind came a woman and two children. These I judged to be the wife and children of the departed. Following came from sixty to seventy aged men and women, hired for the occasion, wailing and moaning, throwing up their hands and venting their sorrow in the most piteous tones, — "O my father! O my mother! O

GATHERING DATES.

the sun! O the moon! O the stars! O the river!"—keeping up the horrible noise until the cortege of death was out of sight.

But I have made this letter lengthy enough, and will affix to it the usual signature.   RIP VAN WINKLE.

IN ASIA MINOR

PALMYRA.

At Alexandria, the master parted from Mr. Goodspeed and began to make inquiries for travelling parties. One day, while visiting the American Consul, he met a gentleman who introduced himself as a fellow-countryman, and said he made one of a party who in a few days would leave for Asia Minor, and gave Rip Van Winkle a pressing invitation to go along with them.

"Is not your party full?" asked the master.

"No."

"How many are there?"

"Three men and two boys, the latter, sons of one of the gentlemen."

"Are all Americans?"

"Yes; one of the gentlemen is from New York, the other two with the boys are from Boston."

"Well, if agreeable to them, I should be glad to join your party."

"I know it will be agreeable, for we have been in quest of two or three more persons to go with us."

"Then count me in."

"We will do so, and it will give us pleasure to come and see you this evening." The master gave the name of his hotel, shook hands with his new friend, and went away to make arrangements for the trip.

"I am in luck," he said to himself, as he reached his room. And so he was. The party with which he connected himself he was destined to find a most congenial one. At night they called upon him, made arrangements with him for the journey, and in a few days in the steamer Corso they were sailing for the Syrian coast. The master wrote:

SMYRNA.

You will expect me to tell you how I got here, and why I came. Finding a pleasant party about to visit Asia Minor I cast in my lot with them, and on board the French steamer Corso, started from Alexandria. We had been out two days when we sighted Jaffa. Though the voyage had been pleasant, the steamer being clean and the company agreeable, we were glad to see the coast again. The nearer I came to the places mentioned in Scripture the more intense became my interest and enthusiasm. Jaffa, you know, is celebrated as the home of Simon Peter, and Dorcas, and also as the port from which Jonah sailed on his perilous visit to Tarshish. It is one of the most ancient cities of Palestine, existing even before Jerusalem, and some say before the flood. It is picturesquely, and beautifully situated on the shore of the blue Mediterranean. As we rode at anchor outside we wondered whether the sights within the city would prove as beautiful as the place viewed from a distance, for looking upon the

JAFFA, FROM THE NORTH.

houses rising one above another, the turrets and minarets pointing to heaven in all directions, the view was a very pleasant one. But we were doomed to disappointment when we entered, and saw the town. The houses are clustered closely together on the hillside, street rises above street, and roof towers above roof, while here and there are seen the tall palms waving their branches, green and slender, as if keeping guard with their long arms over the people below. But like many other things which look well at a distance Joppa (or Jaffa) is a most disgusting place to visit. The streets are narrow and filthy, the houses mean and squalid, and the people indolent and corrupt. A feeling of intense disappointment comes over one who has gazed with admiration on the town from a distance, as he is obliged to pick his way amid filth and rubbish, seeing nothing to please, but everything to disgust him.

Sending our dragoman to obtain some supplies we went on a tour of inspection through the town. Our first inquiry was for the home of Simon the tanner, which we knew to be in existence, but we might as well have inquired for the house that Jack built. Nobody knew anything about Simon the tanner. But by perseverance we discovered the place at length. It is near the sea. A part of the wall remains standing, the house having been carried away piecemeal, by those who wished to retain a relic of the structure. The locality shows that it has been used in ages past for a tannery, though the identity is somewhat doubtful.

Not far from the house of Simon is the tomb of Tabitha. You all know that she was the founder of sewing-circles, a very excellent representative of that much-abused class of people known as "old maids." If she had been a married woman we probably should never have heard of her, but her fame is now in all the churches of Christ. The houses in Jaffa are square stone or plaster buildings, with a flat roof, one or two stories high. I climbed up to the top of one of them, and when there, did not wonder that the people in the evening were accustomed to assemble on the house-top, and that they made it a place of devotion, and even a place for rest and sleep. The houses within are filthy and gloomy, but on the top, with a Syrian sky over-bead, and the Mediterranean sea spread out in front, all was changed. Below us was the wreck of the house in which Simon the tanner once lived, and I thought of that remarkable vision Peter, his guest, had on that roof, in which he saw a sheet let down from heaven, " filled with all manner of four-footed beasts of the earth, and wild beasts, and creeping things, and fowls of the air." I thought of Tabitha, or Dorcas, as Luke calls her, who, when she lay dead, was a theme of wonder and praise on the lips of all the women, who wept, "and showed the garments which Dorcas had made." I thought of that miracle performed by Peter, in which that good woman was recalled to life. I thought that, perhaps, eighteen hundred years ago, that same house where I then was might have been occupied by some Christian family, who came up at evening and looked upon the sea.

As our steamer was to stop a day or two at Jaffa, we concluded to ride inland as far as the town of Ramlah. We started in the afternoon, and our dragoman procured a number of horses for us. They were creatures of all sorts, with wretched saddles and worse bridles. Those who were good horsemen and accustomed to equestrian exercises, at once selected the best animals. It did not matter what kind of a beast I had. I had ridden camels, donkeys, and cows since I had been in the East, and had "done some horsemanship," but up to the time I left home I had seldom been on the back of a horse. Only a year ago I tumbled one horse down when half way up Mount Vesuvius, and it did not make much difference with me what kind of an animal I had. So after the others had made their selection, I took the creature that was left, and a sorry animal he was! The hair had come off in a dozen places, leaving him half bare. The saddle looked as if the rats had been gnawing off its covering, while the bridle was half leather and half cord. Well, I was going to Ramlah, and that was the only way to get there, so I mounted the nag. By touching the reins, and

JAFFA PEARL MERCHANTS.

shouting "ge lang" at the top of my voice, I was able to get him into a dog-trot.

The day was fine, and we rode through an interesting country, olive-trees and immense cactus plants shaded the road. Our way lay across the plain of Sharon, and the narcissus, the orange blossom, and the wild rose grew rank along the way, reminding us of the time when the whole plain, now sandy and desert, bloomed as the garden of God. We passed Gezer, a city formerly of note, of which Horam,

LYDDA.

who was conquered and killed by Joshua, was king; then through the desert of Beth Dagon to Ludd, called in the New Testament Lydda, which is about nine miles from Jaffa. It is still a considerable place, and the ruins of a church built by the Crusaders are so conspicuous, that no traveller riding over the plain fails to stop and gaze about him. St. George, the patron saint of England, was born and buried here. The common story of this saint is that he was a soldier in the army of Diocletian, and suffered martyrdom for the gospel. Edward III.

PLOUGHING IN PALESTINE.

made him the tutelar saint of English chivalry. It was at Lydda that Peter healed the poor paralytic Eneas, who had been bed-ridden eight years. As we paused there that day, where centuries ago the miracle was wrought, we could seem to hear the stern voice of the Galilean fisherman, — " Eneas, Jesus Christ maketh thee whole."

The ride of a few miles brought us to Ramlah, where we were to spend the night. Our baggage and tents having been left in the steamer, our dragomen quartered us in a convent, where we were made as comfortable as could be expected. The approach to this monkish abode was through a narrow road a mile in length, completely overgrown and shaded by the cactus or prickly pear, which grows to immense size. The plant was in full bloom, and its great clusters of flowers hung down to our heads as we rode on beneath them. Through the huge arms of the giant plant, we could see the orange trees in all their beauty, and down through the interlaced foliage shone the beams of the setting sun.

On reaching the convent we were shown about the place, and introduced to the monks, who seemed to be a jolly good-natured set of fellows, who take life less drearily than many persons suppose. A table was set for us, supper served, the ghostly fathers making themselves as handy as the servants in a hotel. At night I was put into a cell, with cold stone floor and walls, a more dreary prison-like place than I ever slept in before. However, I was not at all lonely, for besides one of my friends, who was in the same room, I had the company of innumerable mosquitos that all night long kept buzzing, and innumerable fleas which all night long kept biting. The bed was well enough, what there was of it! It was made for a very small monk, and I am quite a large person. The night was cold, and in vain I tried to make the scanty coverlid reach around me. My friend in the other bed was a man of very different turn of mind from myself. He seldom saw the ludicrous side of anything. In the night he woke. The sombre shadows, the stone walls, the barred windows,

TOWER OF RAMLAH.

all produced in him a feeling of awe, and thinking I might be in the same mental mood, he asked if I was awake, and on receiving an affirmative reply, asked gravely what text I should use if turned suddenly from a pedagogue into a preacher at that impressive hour. At the risk of dissipating his solemnity I was obliged to declare that there was but one passage in the Bible that I thought any preacher could preach from that night — that verse in the book of Isaiah — " For the bed is shorter than that a man can stretch himself on it; and the covering narrower than that he can wrap himself in it."

Early in the morning we rode back to Jaffa, and found the steamer with steam up, and all ready to start, and in an hour after we got on board and were on our way again.

At Tyre we again anchored — ancient Tyre! What its origin was, none can tell, for it is so remote that it is lost to view. We know that Isaiah mentions it as a great city in his time, and Josephus informs us that it was in existence B.C. 1251 years, and Joshua speaks of it as a a strong city two hundred years earlier than that. For a time it was the great commercial city of the world. A complete description of it is found in the twenty-seventh chapter of Ezekiel. From secular history we learn that the inspired description is exact and literal. There were two ports, and they were closed at night by chains being put across the mouth. The population at times was very large, — all engaged in commerce. The modern town has but four hundred inhabitants, and though advantageously located it no more deserves its ancient name — mistress of the sea. Of ancient Tyre little remains. The ruins of an old temple 216 feet long and 136 feet broad, at the dedication of which Eusebius preached, and beneath which rest the remains of Origen and Frederick Barbarossa, with some other fragments, are all that is left. The commerce of Tyre is confined to a few fishing boats, and the beauty of Tyre has been cast into the sea.

We next came to anchor in front of Sidon, but only long enough to throw out some mail bags and discharge a little freight, and we were off again, but we had an excellent sea view of the town.

Soon Beirut was in sight, and we had the pleasure of looking about the great seaport of Syria for some time. The night had been stormy, and with great pleasure we landed and were received by

SIDON.

the American consul and his wife, whom we recognized as old friends. The city has many attractions and seems very much like a European city. Whether you approach it from sea or land, the view is charming. Randall says that the city "contains at least 50,000 inhabitants, of whom about one-third are Mohammedans. There are usually strangers in the city, drawn here for commerce and travel. Many Europeans are settled here, and many European houses adorn the town, and European costumes meet the eye. A large body of French soldiers are now stationed here, the avowed object being the protection of the Christians of the surrounding country from the hostility of the Druses. It is a place of considerable commerce, and large quantities of raw silk are among its exports. The city stands upon quite a promontory, and is most beautifully situated. The old portion of it is densely built, close upon the sea-shore, the streets narrow, crooked, and badly paved. The houses are mostly of stone, substantially built, and have a neat and comfortable appearance. There are many beautiful villas in the suburbs, embowered in groves of mulberry; in fact, the whole country about, as one says, is rapidly becoming one vast mulberry plantation. As you ascend to the upper parts of the town the view becomes magnificent, embracing the Bay of St. George, the distant expanse of the blue sea stretching away in the distance till it blends with the horizon; the heights of Lebanon, rising tier above tier, until, in the far distance, their heads are pinnacled in the clouds, and their 'snowy scalps' glisten in the sunlight. I have seldom looked upon a more extensive, sublime and enchanting landscape than meets the view from the heights of the town back of Beirut."

At Beirut we joined a party of gentlemen who were going to Asia Minor. Some of them were Americans and others were English. Ten of us agreed to go together. The party, before we joined it, had procured servants, dragomen, and guides sufficient for the wants of a much larger party. We were loth to leave Beirut, having found it

BEIRUT.

a very attractive city. The jewelry sellers, the tobacco venders, the hot-coffee boys, the flower dealers, make the streets busy at all hours of the day. Men and women riding about on donkeys presented a novel sight, and the days we were here were filled with incidents of a most pleasant character. Only because we could have the company of a large party, and the services of their dragomen, did we go so soon.

TOBACCO CUTTING.

After leaving Beirut, we came to the Island of Cyprus, a beautiful spot in the Mediterranean sea. Lavnica, its chief town, contains a small population, and has an American consul, who was very civil to us. Here two of us — the Bostonians — were taken with peculiar notions. You know Cyprus is famed for its wines. The grape vintages are very large, and the manufacture of the sparkling fluid is very extensive. A man landing at Cyprus is supposed to be a wine merchant, and he will find at the landing, and at the hotels, drummers who are on hand to show him where the best wines are sold at the lowest price.

The common Cyprus wines taste like rain water that has been standing on tar. But as it is somewhat famous, and very cheap, two of our number determined to buy wine. So they began tasting, tasting, trying the stuff, and when they had tasted and experimented, made their purchase. Well, whether it had any connection with the wine or not, I cannot tell, but the same two men, after buying their wine, concluded to buy a couple of donkeys. Whether they would ever have thought of the donkeys if it had not been for the wine, I cannot tell, but certain I am, that "wine the mocker" and "donkey the kicker" were both contracted for in Cyprus. I asked our friends to let me exhibit the animals when I returned home, to illustrate the productions of Cyprus, but they thought there were American donkeys enough, without introducing any of foreign breed.

Our next stop was at Rhodes, famous for its brazen Colossus, which stood at the entrance of the harbor. It was a statue to Apollo, and was one hundred and five feet high, hollow, and with a winding staircase to the head, from which a view of Asia Minor was obtained. It cost about three hundred and twenty thousand dollars. It stood many years and was shaken down by an earthquake. The metal weighed eight hundred thousand pounds, after lying on the ground nine hundred years. Of course the Colossus was gone, but a beautiful town we saw from the deck of our steamer as we rode at anchor for an hour in the harbor. The name of Rhodes is derived from the number of roses that grow there, the whole island being a perfect bouquet at some seasons of the year.

FLOWERMAN.

The day after we left Rhodes, we passed Patmos, a rock about sixteen miles in circumference, to which the beloved John was banished by the cruel order of Domitian. It looks like a prison, its steep cliffs rising out of the waters of the Egean sea, like the palisades of a vast dungeon. On account of its solitary, dungeon-like aspect, the Romans used it as a prison for convicted criminals. It was the bastile of the Egean, but has become a sacred locality by being made the scene of that prophetic book, which bears the stamp of inspiration in every line.

The next morning we were anchored in the harbor of Smyrna, called by the ancients the " Crown of Ionia," where we were to spend several days. It is a Turkish city, beautifully situated on the side of a hill, which from the water seems to form a complete terrace to the top. We were soon on shore rambling about the place. What we saw may give you a better idea of the town than a particular description. After visiting the American consul we went and paid five francs for the privilege of looking over a few old papers, in hopes to find some American news, but as far as the papers we saw were concerned, no one could tell whether there was such a place as America. The shops in Smyrna are odd places, almost all out of doors. We were amused particularly with the eating-houses. A room in a house, all open in front, had a table or two in the rear, while all the cooking was done in front. Three or four cooks were busily engaged; one making coffee; another frying fish; a third roasting meat. The latter operation was altogether a new one. The fire was in a high perpendicular stove about as large as an eight-inch funnel. The meat was cut about table size, and put upon a piece of stick, making a long string of it. This the man turned round and round with his hands, keeping it as near the red hot stove as possible. As the meat dried he would taste it, and push it down, and when a customer came along he would take off a piece from the lower end of the stick, half done, or double done, as the case might be, and put on another raw piece at the top. There is an advantage to this, for every man sees his own dinner cooked, and knows what he gets.

I visited the slave market in Smyrna. The Christian sentiment even of Turkey has made open public slave auctions unpopular. So the slaves are kept in some old dilapidated house, and those who wish to purchase go there after them. There were about a dozen persons of each sex. The girls were coal-black Nubians, prettily dressed, covered with ornaments, and very tidy. The boys were a far better looking class than our free negroes. They all seemed anxious to be sold, and sat in the windows to display themselves most conspicuously to purchasers. I asked the man who had charge of them the price, and found that it ranged from $200 to $300. I did not buy any.

We happened to be in Smyrna on one of the days when the dervishes perform. These people live in convents like the Catholic

SMYRNA.

monks, and once or twice a week perform. They wear coarse robes, and go about the streets with bare heads, breasts and feet. Sometimes they go dressed in the skins of beasts, and beg or steal as they have opportunity. Some of our company went in on Friday to see them perform. The room of their convent in which they assemble, and admittance to which is secured by the payment of a small sum of money, is designed for this exercise. On a raised platform, or gallery, were the operators. Below, on the floor, were a number of mats, one richer than the rest. At the appointed hour the leader came in and took his seat on the richest mat, and soon he was followed by thirty dervishes, who gathered around him, and reverently kissed his hand as they passed. Then they all knelt together, and the leader repeated in Arabic a sentence which they at once caught from his lips. This was repeated quickly, then more quickly, until it became one broken cry. For about seven minutes they repeated it, swinging their bodies backward and forward as they knelt, with the utmost vehemence. At the end of seven minutes the words or rather sounds, for no words could be distinguished, were changed to another unintelligible sentence which they shouted for five minutes, with increased violence of sound, and the most vehement gesticulations. At the end of the five minutes their eyes began to roll, their features were distorted, and the peculiar trance symptoms began to appear. Then one voice began to sing a plaintive monotonous Arab song; at the end of the first verse they all arose, and joining hands, sang together. This finished they fell into lines, and advanced toward and retreated from each other, with a peculiar sort of a grunt which was most distressing. Then the motion changed to a rapid whirl, the grunting being continued. Soon some began to fall out, wearied and exhausted with the exercise. The others stood up and kept on whirling, until but few remained on their feet. Then the leader gave a signal at which they came to a sudden pause, and striking up a dirge-like wail left the room. The whole performance is very disgusting and unintelligible; and is witnessed with pain.

While wandering about Smyrna, one day, we fell in with a rich old Jew whose name was Daniel. He invited us to his house, and introduced us to his wife and children. One of the girls was but thirteen years old, and had been married two years. A daughter at the age of twelve was to be married the next month. We asked him how many daughters he had, and he replied that if he had as many daughters as sons they would ruin him. We asked him why, and he told us that he gave £200 or $1,000 to the man who married the girl, and spent $1,000 more in ornaments. He showed us the necklace and bracelets which he had bought for the girl so soon to be married. They were very elegant and costly. We were told by him that some Jewish official goes about making matches between the boys and girls,

WATER BOY OF SMYRNA.

the bargain being made with the parents and not with the parties themselves, the young folks not being consulted in the case.

The old man, with his flowing robe and his long white beard, sitting among his children, was well calculated to remind us of the ancient patriarchs who traded away their sons and daughters as custom, caprice or convenience suggested.

We went out to see the tomb of Polycarp one day. It is on the hill overlooking the town, and a stately palm-tree waves over it. The old martyr has ascended to his reward.

EPHESUS.

This once populous city is now a mass of ruins. Here where Paul preached and the Great Diana was worshipped, is nothing but desolation and decay, and the traveller feels a sensation of profound sadness, as he makes his way among the remains of former greatness.

The city is very ancient. It is situated at the mouth of the Cayster, and was at one time a great centre of commerce. We find traces of it for more than ten centuries before the Christian era. The name of the place figures in art, literature, commerce and religion. The temple of its deity, Artemis, was one of the wonders of antiquity. On the night Alexander the Great was born, this temple was set on fire by an incendiary named Erostratus, his object being to make his name famous. In this he failed, for very few persons know anything of his exploit. Only a fool expects to become famous by a great crime. The temple was rebuilt. The women as well as the men of Ephesus vied with each other to make great sacrifices for this purpose. The reconstructed edifice was Ionic in its architecture, and was a marvel of style and finish. It was regarded as one of the seven wonders of the world. Artemis was the famous Diana, who was such an object of interest to the silversmiths and shrine-makers of Ephesus at the time Paul went there to preach. The attributes and powers of this goddess were supposed to be wonderful, but she has not saved her chief city from destruction.

Within a few years, vigorous explorations have been made, which show that the accounts of the former splendor of the place have not been exaggerated. "I commenced," says Mr. J. T. Wood, "by exploring the great theatre which is now called St. Paul's Theatre by the Greeks, and which is undoubtedly the theatre mentioned in the New Testament. It was a grand building of the ancient city, and was raised on the western lope of Mount Covessus, within a few hundred yards of which was situated the city port. The outer diameter of the

PLAIN OF EPHESUS.

theatre was four hundred and ninety-five feet, and it was capable of seating twenty-four thousand five hundred persons. It had a splendid proscenium, adorned with two tiers of columns, and at each end of this there was an entry for those persons of high rank, the vestal virgins, and others who were entitled to places on the lowermost seats nearest the stage. It must have been at one of the entrances that St. Paul struggled with his friends who succeeded in preventing his entrance into the theatre, on the occasion of the uproar caused by Demetrius and his fellow-craftsmen, or it might have been at the foot of one of the slopes, probably the southern one, which led up steep ascents from the road to the entrances."

The tomb of St. Luke, now in ruins, a circular building, fifty feet in diameter, is here. Though Luke did not die, nor was he buried in Ephesus, the tomb, which in its time was an elaborate structure, is an object of considerable interest. There are also ruins of churches, public buildings, private residences, but the stamp of desolation is on them all. The city, or what is left of it, lies on the plain like a fallen queen, while silence broods where once was activity and life.

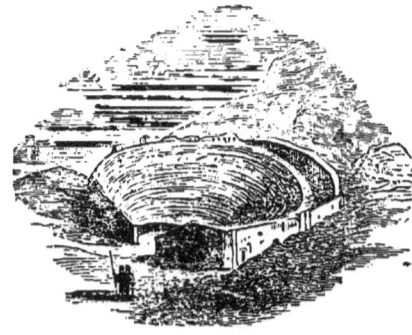

EPHESIAN AMPHITHEATRE.

One of the churches, now in ruins, bears the name of St. Luke. Mr. Wood thinks it was formerly dedicated to that Evangelist, but it is more likely that it derived its name from being located near what is said to be the tomb of St. Luke. These churches show that Christianity obtained great wealth and influence, and that the original builders of these places of public worship were not stinted in their means, nor narrow in their idea of architectural elegance.

The people of Ephesus are as fallen as the city. With few exceptions they are a wretched class, who live among the ruins, and rob all they can. They obtain a scanty living by raising swine, tilling the earth, and fleecing travellers. Whether on the plain or on the hills, Prion and Covessus, the same poverty and degradation are seen. The woe fell not only on the church but on the city. The candlestick has been removed out of its place, and Ephesus is a mound of elegant fragments of a once renowned emporium of wealth and fashion. It is sad to look about upon the sepulchres of departed greatness. The great heroes

RUINS OF EPHESUS.

and statesmen have been forgotten. Their names are also lost. They are, with a few rare exceptions, unmentioned in history. They might have been as ambitious as the man who set fire to the temple, that his name and fame might rise parallel with that of the goddess Diana. The members of the council condemned him to death, and decreed that his name should never again be mentioned. But theirs, like his, are forgotten.

The image of Diana, in the temple, was a small ebony statue, which was supposed to have fallen down from Jupiter, and as such, was worshipped by the multitude.

Paul first visited Ephesus A. D. 54, while he was on his journey to Jerusalem. At that time he saw the degradation of the people. He hastened to Jerusalem, completed his business, and returned to Ephesus, where he abode three years. At times he had the companionship and co-operation of Gaius, Aristarchus, Timothy, Erastus and Titus. He at once organized his church of twelve disciples. But soon trouble arose. The silversmiths of Ephesus, who had gained a living by the manufacture of little silver images of Diana, an article that was in great demand, found that this revival had spoiled their business. Their trinkets would not sell, and they held a mass meeting, made confusion, created an uproar, and set the whole city in a blaze.

About the beginning of the third century, Constantine ascended the throne of the Roman empire, and has been styled "the first Christian emperor." He had seen the folly of paganism, and on his accession to the throne in 306, he resolved to make Christianity the religion of his empire. His conversion, as related by Eusebius, was a sort of miracle. "He was marching at the head of his army from France into Italy, on an expedition which he knew fully involved all his future destiny. Oppressed with extreme anxiety, he looked for aid of some deity. About noon one day, while engaged in prayer, a luminous cross appeared in the clouds, brighter than the sun. On it was inscribed

In hoc signo vinces (by this sign thou shalt conquer). While he pondered, an angel appeared to him, and bade him make the cross the symbol of his nation, and inscribe it on all his armor. This pious deception was practised to influence the minds of credulous Christians and win them over in a body to his standard. He succeeded, and was no sooner seated on his throne than he began to rebuild the churches, and pass laws for the protection of Christians. Christianity became the established religion of the empire, the road to preferment and honor. But religion by this time had become very corrupt, and the Ephesian church, founded by Paul, and for a long time under the pastoral charge of the apostle John, began to decline. The city is a devastation. Its once gorgeous temples are mounds of ruins, and some traces of a wall, with a solitary watchtower, are all that remains of Ephesus.

"A more thorough change can scarcely be conceived than that which actually occurred. Once the seat of active commerce, the very sea has shrunk from its solitary shores; its streets, once populous with the devotees of Diana, are now ploughed over by the Ottoman serf, or browsed by the sheep of the peasant. It was early the stronghold of Christianity, and stands at the head of the apostolic churches of Asia. Not a single Christian now dwells within it; its mouldering arches and dilapidated walls merely whisper the tale of its glory; and it requires the acumen of the geographer, and the active scrutiny of the exploring traveller, to form a probable conjecture as to the actual site of the first wonder of the world."

Dr. Chandler, who visited Ephesus long ago, says, — "The inhabitants are a few Greek peasants, living in extreme wretchedness, dependence, and insensibility; the representatives of an illustrious people, and inhabiting the wreck of their greatness — some, the substructure of the glorious edifices which they raised, some beneath the vaults of the stadium, once the crowded scene of their diversions. We heard the partridge call in the area of the theatre and of the stadium. The glorious pomp of its heathen worship is no longer remembered; and Christianity, which was there nursed by apostles and fostered by general councils, until it increased to fulness of stature, barely lingers on in an existence hardly visible. On approaching it from the wretched village of Aiasalouk, a few scattered fragments of antiquity occur; and on the hill above, some traces of the former walls, and a solitary watchtower, mark the extent of the city."

> " Where is Diana's temple ? — Where the shout
> Of many people like the deep-voic'd sea,
> 'Great is the Ephesian Goddess ! '
>   — Scan the dust
> That gathers o'er thy feet, — and point me out
> One glittering particle of that proud dome,
> And those rich columns, gift of throned kings —
> Where is the altar at whose costly shrine
> All Asia worshipped in that idol's praise
> Which fell from Jupiter ?
>   Thou canst not tell ! —
> *World! do thy wonders pass away so soon?*
>
>   — I pause, — but none reply,
> Save where the Cayster with retreating wave
> Moans round some sullen rock, — or from his pool
> With rushes dank, the lonely bittern screams.
> — Where art thou, Ephesus ? — I hear a voice
> As from the hollow grave, — " Go, search God's book,
> And when thou mark'st its fearful threat fulfill'd
> Upon these lifeless plains, — look to thine heart
> And see if aught doth rankle there, to tempt
> The Righteous Judge in sorrow's night to shroud
> Thy 'golden candlestick. ' — If so, repent !
> Do the first works, — to thy first love return, —
> And on these ruins date thy deathless gain."
>
>   PERGAMOS.

Pergamum, good authorities say, the real name of the place should be. This is an inland town, twenty-two miles from the sea, and is on the banks of the Caicus, at its junction with the Selmas. The ancient town was located between two hills, on one of which the Acropolis was burnt. It must in its day have been a place of great beauty, and its relics show a high state of art on the part of its inhabitants. The remains of an amphitheatre scarcely inferior to that at

PERGAMOS.

Ephesus, the fragments of one or two churches, with extensive ruins of other public and private edifices, fill up the valley and seem to mourn over the devastations which have come upon the city and its inhabitants. The ancient city was renowned for its culture and refinement.

One or two extensive libraries were found there, and in the ancient world of letters, Pergamos held a high place. A Christian church was planted in this city at a very early date, and for a time it flourished, but soon became corrupt, and when John was commanded to write to the "angels" or ministers of the churches in Asia, the church in Pergamos was overwhelmed with corruption and false doctrines. Little is known of the church, except that it grew more and more corrupt, and was finally extinguished. The name of the city is said to come from Pergamus, who slew a Teuthranian king and took his territory. It has been ruled by Persians, Romans, and Syrians, and has a checkered history, until now its name is a byword and reproach.

THYATIRA.

This is the ancient name of the modern town, Ak-hissar, which means "White Castle." It is a ten days' horseback ride from Pergamos to this place, but every hour of the ride is through a region of wild beauty which makes it anything but tiresome. In the early days Thyatira was celebrated for its dyes and dyers. It was a great place for this branch of business, and traces of it are yet found. The church here was probably planted by Lydia. She was baptized by the Apostle Paul at Philippi, having there become a convert to the Christian faith. Returning to her home with her household, which was probably composed of the servants and tradespeople who went with her to help her sell her goods, she organized the church, which seems never to have been greatly prospered, and which soon became corrupt and extinct. As a woman planted the church, so a woman corrupted it. "That woman Jezebel" wrought much misery, and the church was denounced because she was allowed to teach. The present population of the town is somewhat thriving. Signs of industry are seen. The mosque of St. John, once a Christian temple, is still an elegant structure. The products of the place are cotton and grain, which are cultivated in comparatively large quantities. Ar

" inn " of great cleanliness and quiet is found here, and, to a traveller hungry and tired, this is not one of the least recommendations of the place. The towns in Asia Minor are sadly destitute of this luxury, and the one we found in Thyatira was a great aid to our comfort.

AK HISSAR.

SARDIS.

Sart is the present name. A ride of about forty or fifty miles brings us to this seat of one of the ancient churches, on the slopes of Mount Tmolus. Through it flowed the river Pactolus, and all around are the ruins of the once elegant city. There are the remains of temples, the marble arches and pillars, and the broken remnants of great buildings. There is a terrible sense of desolation over everything. You are conscious, as you sit on the broken stones, that you are in the sepulchre of a great and renowned city. The Turkish village is thriving, but it does not break the monotony nor drive away the sadness. The theatre and the stadium show their outlines, while the remains of the churches tell us to some extent what Sardis was in the days of Christ. The Acropolis, whose walls still stand, was the great attraction of the place. But nothing else now remains but undistinguishable ruins and the Turkish hamlet, with a few pillars of the ruined temple of Cybele, to tell of a city that opened its arms to welcome the gospel, but proved unworthy of its blessings.

PHILADELPHIA.

Not the city of William Penn, between the Delaware and the Schuylkill, but Allah Shehr (City of God), about thirty miles from Sardis. This is the best preserved of all the seven cities to whom special messages were sent by John. The city was built by and named for Attalus Philadelphus, and is situated on an arm of Mount Tmolus. It has suffered much from earthquakes, and one of these dire convulsions during the reign of Tiberius, in the seventeenth year of the Christian era, nearly destroyed the place, but it rose again, and became an opulent and wealthy city, and so continued for many years. The present town has more than a thousand inhabitants, and is an interesting spectacle from any of its approaches. Christian worship, corrupted to be sure, has been maintained here from the days of the apostles. There are five or more places of worship in this little village, and the tide of Mohammedanism is stoutly and successfully resisted. One church now standing is a structure supposed to have been one of the early buildings erected by the primitive church, and it may be that apostles preached within its walls.

However, there is not much of interest to the traveller, who soon

TEMPLE OF CYBELE, SARDIS.

sees all there is of the place, and is glad to be gone. Gibbon, speaking of the seven churches, and the cities in which they were located, says, —" Philadelphia alone has been saved by prophecy, or courage. At a distance from the sea, forgotten by the Europeans, encompassed on all sides by the Turks, her valiant citizens defended their religion and freedom above fourscore years, and at length capitulated with the proudest of the Ottomans. Among the Greek colonies and churches of Asia, Philadelphia is still erect, — a column in a scene of ruins, — a pleasing example that the paths of honor and safety may sometimes be the same."

There has been little change in Philadelphia for a long time. But modern views seem to be encroaching, and probably those views, acted out in the interest of commerce, may save it from the entire ruin which time has brought on Sardis and Laodicea. Already the sound of the rushing steam train is heard in Asia Minor, and the heavy tread of the later day is heard on the ancient plains, awakening them to enterprise and vitality.

LAODICEA.

Eski-hissar, — this means "Old Castle," and is the modern name of ancient Laodicea. The city was famed eighteen centuries ago for its vast wealth. It was the great mart of that country. It was a city of banks and bankers, and drew to it men of means.

What Gibbon said of the place is literally true. "The circus and the stately theatres of Laodicea are now peopled with wolves and foxes." The ruins of the old gymnasium are mounds and piles of broken fragments that no antiquarian can assort or put together. Poverty reigns all round, and the woe of God has fallen on the city of bankers and merchants who once boasted of their gold and fine raiment.

It would make my letter too long to tell of the other places visited. I wanted to cross over into Armenia, and dash over the plain of Babylon, or stroll about awhile among the ruins of Nineveh,

PHILADELPHIA.

or look upon Mount Ararat, on the top of which the ark rested, but my travelling companions cannot take the trip. Ever since I read Layard's researches at Nineveh I have felt a strong desire to see the famous city to which Jonah was sent on his perilous venture, but must forego the pleasure at this time. More than any other city of the remote past, has Nineveh contributed to the department of archæology, and thrown light upon the manners, customs and peoples of other ages. Nor do any other cities so show the literal fulfilment of scripture as these two, — Babylon on the Euphrates, and Nineveh on the Tigris. It seems as if the builders of those two cities were charged with writing on the stones and bricks of the very foundations a history which should last until the end of the world, and be read by the curious and the wise after thousands of years had rolled over the human family. Babylon speaks of Nebuchadnezzar from the tower of Ben Hassan to Birs Nimroud, while Nineveh is eloquent in every vestige of a city that for ages was hidden from the eyes of men, but now comes out of its sepulchre to be an impressive record of Providence and an accurate fulfilment of prophecy.

RIP VAN WINKLE.

BIRS NIMROUD.

IN DAMASCUS.

DAMASCUS.

AFTER the visit to Asia Minor, which included many spots seen, of which no mention is made in the letters of Rip Van Winkle to his boy friends, the party turned back toward the sea, and the master wrote next from Damascus.

DAMASCUS.

Damascus is one of the oldest cities on the globe. Its history is lost in the dim haze of remote antiquity. It had even in the long-ago times of the patriarch Abraham become an influential and populous place. Josephus informs us that it was founded by Uz, the great grandson of Noah, and we have no reason to dispute the statement. The city is referred to by Isaiah, who says, "The head of Syria is Damascus." One of the stewards of Abraham's household, Eleazar, abode here. One of the most marked subjects of miraculous clemency lived here — Naaman. One of the most noted of the apostles commenced his ministry at Damascus, and went out of the gate at which he had been converted, praising God. For perennial beauty, for excellence of location, for brilliant history and scenery, Damascus has few rivals. Its ancient history is interwoven with the names of Benhadad and Hazael; its modern history is connected with those ever-conquering Romans, and the fanatical Moslems. The city has been in the hands of the Babylonians, the Persians, the Greeks, the Romans, the Saracens, and the Turks, but it lies to-day beneath a Syrian sun, a miracle of beauty.

It is said that Mohammed once came within sight of Damascus, and after gazing long on its beautiful outlines, turned away, and when asked why he did not enter, replied that a man could have but one paradise, and that his must be in the future. The prophet could have paid no more striking tribute to the beauty of Damascus than this.

Striking the Abana, a beautiful stream, now running slowly along, then surging with great velocity, now spreading wide upon a pebbly bed, then channelled between rocks that have been worn to perfect smoothness; now gliding beneath vines and fig-trees, and arches of flowers, and anon pouring forth into crystal sunlight, and sparkling with wonderful beauty, I never had an appreciation of Naaman's feelings until I saw Abana. No wonder he asked, "Are not Abana and Pharpar, rivers of Damascus, better than all the waters of Israel?"

Peeping through a cut in Anti-Lebanon, we gaze down on Damascus five hundred feet below us. Enveloped in foliage, rich, green, and golden, extending for miles, backed by forests of cedar, with its hundred and fifty thousand inhabitants, its countless mosques and minarets glittering in the setting sun, beaming with beauty and dazzling to the eye, was the city we had come so far to see.

On entering Damascus, which we did in a long procession, single file, we found that we were not among friends. The scowling Moslems came out and looked at us as we walked our horses through their streets, and the Turkish soldiers lounging in the street seemed scarcely willing to clear the way before us.

We found the Hotel de Palmyra in the street called "Straight," the Via Recta of the ancient Romans. This is doubtless the same street to which Ananias was sent, to inquire in "the house of Judas, for one Saul of Tarsus." It is now a narrow lane, crowded with houses and stores, very crooked, and running the whole length of the city. It was once a broad street, with noble colonnades, forming three grand avenues through the city, and was lined with noble abodes. The pillars of these colonnades have left their marks, and the street has grown narrower and narrower, according to Turkish customs, until in scarcely any part of it could two carriages stand abreast. The street is about one mile and an eighth in length, the houses mostly covered with thatched roof and matting, and it is quite as dismal as Via Dolorosa in Jerusalem.

The Hotel de Palmyra is a venerable old structure, encircling an open square, into which all the apartments enter, light and ventilation being secured from within, rather than from without. The outside of the hotel resembles a high, rough, windowless wall. In the centre of the square court within is a marble fountain, beneath the falling jets of which the goldfish were sporting and the lilies were growing. The apartments were originally finished in a style of great Oriental magnificence. I doubt not that the antique carvings in the room where I slept would cost as much as a respectable house in New York or Boston. In that hotel we had a grand illustration of Oriental suppers. The table was set in an alcove looking out upon the court and the fountain. Huge candelabras were on the table, and numerous wax candles sent a cheerful light and a grateful perfume around the place. There was indeed something romantic in the whole scene. The table loaded with beautiful flowers; the candles lighting up the heavy carv-

PUBLIC GARDEN, DAMASCUS.

ings; the water gurgling and glittering in the gloomy rays of light; the black servants, in long, flowing oriental robes, moving noiselessly about; and the shadowy appearances that seemed to come and go with the flickering beams, all added to the mystery of the hour.

A peculiarity of the table-serving is that the articles, which are very numerous, are all served on separate dishes. A little bit of meat is served first. Then, when that is eaten, the plate is whipped away and a vegetable is put in its place, and with all our ingenuity at Damascus we could not get what we wanted to eat, meat and vegetables on the same plate. A dozen or twenty courses are set, and you rise from the table hungry. There is a parade of nothing but dishes and dessert, fruit being very plenty. To have a dinner served in English style is an impossibility.

And now let us go about Damascus. We put ourselves in the hands of Abu Ibrahim, an old Jew who acts as guide and cicerone to strangers. He had so served many Americans, and their old tattered, greasy recommendations he exhibited with much delight. The old man took us first to the bazaars, a famous institution in all Eastern cities. I may as well describe them. They are much alike, varying from each other only in richness and extent. They are long streets or avenues, covered with matting or roof, pierced so as to admit the light. These avenues are lined on both sides with little stalls, some ten feet wide in front and from four to ten feet deep. They are devoted to all the trades, and to every variety of ware. Some of them are so shallow that they serve only as a show case, while the proprietor is obliged to sit outside; and some of them are deep enough for the craftsmen to be at work inside. These market places are gaudy and fascinating in the extreme. An Arab always runs to the bazaar. Ask a cicerone what there is to see in Cairo, Damascus or Constantinople, and he will begin the enumeration of objects with the bazaars. Ask a dragoman what he can show you, and he will tell you, " The

STREET IN DAMASCUS.

bazaars." Whichever way he starts with you, he is always sure to bring you to the fancy exchange. These little shops contain all sorts of traffic. In one of them the silversmiths will be at their work; in another the cabinetmakers will be making antique furniture, boxes inlaid with pearl, and chairs sparkling with tinsel and gilt; in another shoes are sold; black shoes and white shoes; red shoes and green shoes; yellow shoes and drab shoes; shoes with gold spangles and silver spangles; shoes for little feet and shoes for big feet; shoes for matrons and shoes for maids — all sorts of shoes; in another all sorts of upholstery and needle-work are shown, very tempting to Turkish ladies, as it would be to American ladies; in another all the branches of the saddler's trade are exhibited — beautiful Turkish saddles, gay bridles, and all the decorations of that noble creature, the horse; in another are all sorts of tin ware, from a tin trumpet to a tin ventilator; in another we find toys and trinkets for boys and girls, jumping jacks, and gimcracks, in vast variety. The goods are showily arranged, and the keeper asks about four times as much as he expects to get. If you ask the price of a pair of shoes, and he says twenty francs, you may calculate on getting them at about five francs.

The next place to which the guide took us was the great mosque, into which we were allowed to look, but were not permitted to enter. This mosque is very ancient, and there is proof that it was the famous house of the god Rimmon which was in existence as long ago as the days of Naaman the Syrian. It has a minaret two hundred and fifty feet high, called the "Minaret of Jesus." The Mohammedans say that, when Christ comes to judge the world, he will sit on this pinnacle. Built for a heathen god, when Christianity subdued the world, this pagan temple was dedicated to Christ. Over a former gateway of this mosque is a cross with the inscription, — "Thy kingdom, O Christ, is an everlasting kingdom, and Thy dominion endureth throughout all generations." There it stands, and there it will stand until the Koran shall be banished, and Christ shall be enthroned again in this ancient house of Rimmon. It is claimed that, in a little sanctuary under the mosque is kept the head of John the Baptist. "Historians tell us that Khâled visited the cathedral after the capture of the city, and insisted on obtaining admission to the sacred cave. On descending he found a small vault with an altar, on which was laid the casket. Upon it was an inscription in Greek, to the following effect: 'This casket contains the head of John the Baptist, son of Zachariah.'"

But the most interesting and most melancholy thing I saw at Damascus was the Maronite section of that city. About twenty years ago, occurred those fearful outbreaks in which so many of the Maronites were slaughtered by the Mohammedan Druses. At the beginning of the year 1860, there lived in Damascus about twenty-eight thousand Maronites or Christians, a class of people who rejected the teachings of Mohammed. The rest of the population, with the exception of a few thousand Jews, were Druses and Mohammedans. Throughout the northern part of Syria the Druses and Maronites are found, and they cordially hate each other. In the early part of the year 1860, the war which had long been threatening between the two factions broke out. The Druses had the sympathy of all Mohammedans, and even the Turkish troops sided with them, and, thus assisted, they entered upon the remorseless murder of the Christians, as the Maronites were called. All over Syria deeds of blood were perpetrated, villages burned, men, women and children murdered. Not only at Damascus, but at Aleppo and Hamath, and all the inland cities, blood flowed in torrents. Even the Franks and the missionaries were killed, whenever they fell into the cruel hands of the Druses.

The poor Maronites were slaughtered like sheep. One hundred and sixty towns were burnt; ten thousand men were killed, and twenty-five thousand women were sold into slavery. For a time after the outbreak commenced, the Christians in Damascus were not molested, but soon the storm broke out. Two thousand four hundred were killed, and the rest expelled, leaving their houses and property to the plunderers. The slaughter was terrible. Men were divested of their clothing and pinioned to the walls of houses in the form of a cross; dead bodies were piled up in the streets, and nothing left undone to make the massacre terrible beyond description. The savage Moslems and the Turkish soldiers, entering the houses of the Maronites, would commit every abuse upon the women, and then murder them; little babes were caught from the couch and dashed to pieces against the marble walls, on which the blood still remains.

Just beyond the quarter once occupied by the Christians is an old leper hospital, said to have been the city residence of Naaman. The house from the window of which Paul was let down is shown. It is a wonder they have not kept the veritable bucket.

We were in Damascus five days, and then were glad to get away as we could. The night before we started, the pasha confiscated our horses, and only by the most strenuous efforts of the American consul did we get them. We were off before the pasha or people were up, and not one of us felt safe until a dozen miles were between us and the city.

In our rambles outside of the city, we saw some of the cedars of Lebanon. The groves are beautiful, and furnish shade for travellers, and concealment from the nomadic tribes that seek them as a refuge from law and justice. It is not very safe for a small party to be found in them. They are likely to be robbed of all they have.

After leaving Damascus we visited Baalbec, that wonderful city of ruins at the foot of Anti-Libanus. Baalbec is called by the Greeks Heliopolis, the city of the sun. In its day, it must have been well worthy of the name. For hundreds of years it has been in ruins. In visiting Baalbec, says Dr. Thompson, the "first impression of disappointment runs rapidly into admiration and wonder. You go to the end of a prostrate column, and are almost startled to find that, on tiptoe. and with the hand at utmost stretch, you cannot measure its diamter! You climb in between two of those standing columns, and feel

CEDARS OF LEBANON.

instantly dwarfed into an infant. Looking up to the entablature with a shudder, you wonder how big it may be. A fragment lies at the base; you leap down and measure. It is fourteen feet thick! And such fragments and such columns are all around, and block up your way. Little by little, and with difficulty, you grasp the grand design, and, going out eastward into the centre of the broad platform, take your stand in front of the main entrance. With those six pillars to help your imagination, you reconstruct the whole noble edifice, with twenty such giants on a side! and there you may be safely left much longer than we have time to wait for you. It is growing

BAALBEC.

late, and the subject tedious. If you want to study either Baalbec or Palmyra in detail, I commend you to the magnificent drawings of Wood and Dawkins. They visited Baalbec in 1751; but, though thus old, they are far more elaborate and minute than any others. Of written descriptions there are countless numbers, but the only way to become really possessed of Baalbec is to visit, explore, and study it for yourself."

The immense size of the stones used by the builders of Baalbec strikes every beholder with wonder. Dr. Thompson says that these stones were quarried in different ages. "The most ancient," he says, "are the foundations seen on the west and north sides of the great temple to which the six columns belonged. The first tier above ground consists of stones of different lengths, but all about twelve and a half feet thick, and the same in width. Then came over these stones, more than sixty-three feet long, the largest blocks, perhaps, that were ever placed in a wall by man. One of this class lies in the quarry, where it can be viewed all round, and measured easily. It is fourteen by seventeen, and sixty-nine feet long." Dr. Robinson, who, Dr.

FALLEN PILLAR.

Thompson says, " is the greatest master of measuring tape in the world," gives the dimensions of three stones thus: "One is sixty-four feet long, another sixty-three feet eight inches, and the remaining one sixty-three feet; the whole, one hundred and ninety feet eight inches; the height about thirteen feet, and the thickness perhaps greater." You will, of course, ask about the machinery with which the ancients hauled such stones as these. But no one can tell you much about that. You must search among the "Lost Arts" for the wonderful enginery that must have been employed. The more I see of the cities of other days, the more am I impressed with the magnitude of the loss the human family has sustained in some of its ages from the dropping out of scientific facts and formulas, mechanical appliances, and artistic skill.

From Baalbec to the Cedars! From art to nature! From man to God!

RIP VAN WINKLE.

IN GALILEE.

GENNESARETH.

THE reader will now be asked to accompany our traveller through the Holy Land. The boys are waiting to receive the letter, but we will read it before the master seals it up and sends it away.

TIBERIAS.

Leaving Damascus, we struck across the mountains of Lebanon and the wild country which intervened, and after hard horseback riding and much delay, reached the head waters of the Sea of Galilee, now and then getting sight of the historical mountains, as they towered toward the sky. Hermon the Great, and Little Hermon, Gilead, and Tabor show themselves, while, now and then, the great head of Carmel, off by the sea, is seen, or imagined among the cloud lands.

We reach Chorazin, now known as Tell Hûm, in every stone of which we seem to hear a divine woe pronounced. Here we find some ruins said to be older than any in Palestine. What the edifice was used for none can tell, but it marks an order of architecture such as is seldom found in the Holy Land. "The extent," says Dr. Robinson, " of the foundations of this structure is no longer definitely to be made out. We measured one hundred and five feet along the northern wall, and eighty feet along the western; perhaps this was their whole length. Within the space thus enclosed, and just around, are

MAGDALA.

strewed, in utter confusion, numerous columns of compact limestone, with beautiful Corinthian capitals, sculptured entablatures, ornamental friezes, and the like. The pedestals of the columns are often still in their place, though sometimes overturned and removed."

The next village on the shore is Magdala. The place, as we rode through it, looked as if the seven devils cast out of Mary still lived here in quiet possession of the town.

Leaving Magdala, we rode through groves of magnificent oleanders and magnolias, which, higher than the horse's head, are in full bloom, and we are obliged to crush them down to ride along.

A mile or two on we came to Beth Arbel, a little, mean village on the shore. Then descending to the water's edge, we ride beneath some high bluffs, full of caves, in which lurking robbers now make their homes. In the time of Herod the Great, lawless bandits filled these caves, and they became so numerous as to demand the attention of the government; and so strong were they, that for a long time they defied military power. Herod lowered men down from the high cliffs above, and they threw themselves upon the robbers, or hurled arrows at them, and destroyed them. In this way, the caves were cleared of these dangerous men who had long infested them, and from that time became the abodes of peaceful hermits, who subsisted on the fish of the lake and the berries of the hill. There are rooms for five hundred men to live in these caves comfortably and securely.

Tiberias is located close to the shore of the lake, and is still a somewhat populous city. When we reached, after a hard ride, our tents, which were pitched on a rising ground overlooking the waters, it seemed to me that I had hardly ever seen a view more beautiful and inspiring. The whole region is one of surpassing loveliness. No wonder Christ often resorted to the Sea of Galilee. In his day, it must have been a place of wonderful attractions. The city of Tiberias, which now contains but twenty-five hundred inhabitants, was founded by Herod Antipas, and though hardly mentioned in scripture, has figured largely in profane history. The lake is a basin of water, egg-shaped, thirteen miles long, and six miles wide. The river Jordan flows through the sea, rushing on its resistless course, keeping up its own distinct hues, until it pours out at the other end. The banks on the west side slope somewhat gradually to the water's edge, but over on the east side they are precipitous, two hundred feet high, destitute of verdure, and looking sombre and gray in the light of the summer's sun. When Christ lived, several fine cities were on the western shore of the sea, but they have disappeared one by one, Tiberias alone remaining. We spent one night here, bathed in the sea, and early the next morning took a scow, and had a voyage, half way between a row and a sail, on the lake. To illustrate the want of energy and industry, I may state that though there are thousands of inhabitants on the shores of the sea, and every attraction to lead them out upon its waters, there is but one boat of any kind on this part of the lake, and that would be hardly deemed safe to cross a river a hundred yards wide in our country. The sea is full of fish, but there is no enterprise at boat building. Yankee enterprise or British capital would soon cover it with steamboats and yachts.

The people, who subsist on fish, have two or three ways of taking them. The most common way is to feed them with chloride of mercury, of which they eat and die, float to the shore, are gathered and taken to market. Another way is for a naked man to go out into the lake, and stand perfectly still, and when he sees in the crystal waters a fellow that he wants, he throws his net over him, and one time in a hundred gets him.

I have told you that we had two boys in our company. On the morning of our arrival, the youngsters, while sitting on a rock overlooking the sea, had some half angry and half playful contest of words which resulted in a foolish attempt to jostle each other while close to the edge, the result of which was they were both thrown into the lake. They cried lustily for help, and though they both knew how to swim, as all boys should, they would have drowned if we had not been at hand to fish them out. They looked like drowned rats, and were greatly ashamed of themselves.

We rode from Tiberias to Mount Tabor, supposed to be the scene of the Transfiguration. There may be doubt as to this being the veritable place, but it seems as if made by God for just such a transaction. It is about fourteen hundred feet above the plain, is conical in form, and the ascent is sharp and tedious. There are caves in the

ARAB STORY TELLER.

wooded sides inhabited by hermits, who seldom, if ever, go to the villages below. From the top a glorious view is obtained, and well was I repaid for climbing. The lookout is grand. Yonder in the sunlight reposes the Sea of Galilee. Along the country runs the Jordan in its tortuous course! Lebanon, Carmel, Gilead, and Hermon, are all in view. In troublous times, Tabor is infested with robbers, and some of them we saw sitting on their horses, gazing at us from a distance.

An incident occurred when I was on the top of Tabor which well nigh finished my journey before I desired. I had dismounted, and was walking along behind my horse in a somewhat thoughtless way. To quicken his pace I brushed a twig, which I carried in my hand, across his legs, which, instead of having the intended effect, caused him to dash his heels in my face, and I went backwards to the earth quicker by far than I can tell the story, seeing more stars than my gracious Father has ever placed in the heavens. My friends thought that was the end of me, and for a moment I thought so myself. However, I only received a few scratches and a lame rib.

Leaving Tabor, we ride to the wells of Lubieh, and then to Hattin, or Horns of Hattin, a hill resembling the horns on the saddle of a camel, and said to be the Mount of Beatitudes, where Christ preached his discourse recorded in the book of Matthew. It may have been the Mount, or it may have received the honor from the fact that a man speaking on its sides would have a noble place from which to address a vast multitude so that all could hear. A little beyond is the plain where Saladin overwhelmed the Crusaders, annihilating their last hope of dominion in Palestine.

NAZARETH.

Late one afternoon we reached this town and encamped on a plain below the town, which is built on the side of a hill in a most delightful and picturesque way. The town looks beautiful at a distance, and when entered is found to be, unlike many other Eastern cities, cleanly and cheerful. There are about thirty-five hundred inhabitants, industrious and thrifty people. This, of course you know, was the scene of Christ's boyhood and early manhood. To this place his parents came on their return from Egypt, here he worked at his

A WOMAN OF NAZARETH.

trade, and associated with the young men who afterward beheld his mighty works. Every rock and hill, every valley and dell, must have been familiar to him, and rendered sacred by his footsteps.

When we had rested a little, we went up to the town, feeling a wonderful interest at every step. Beneath the Latin convent we were shown the "Grotto of the Annunciation," as it is termed. Leaving the church above, where a service is being performed, we pass down over a flight of fifteen steps into the cave where the angel communicated to the Virgin Mary the fact that she should immediately become the mother of the world's Master. The kitchen, fireplace, and chimney of the Virgin's subterranean house are pointed out. The monks say that the roof of this cave is miraculously suspended in the air, and show us a pillar which they say the infidels hacked through to let the roof down, but instead of falling it remained suspended by miraculous power. We then go to the shop where Christ is said to have wrought at his trade, in which is an ancient table which they say he made, and from which he often ate and drank with his early friends and disciples. A very clumsy table it is, but not more clumsy than the lies the monks tell about it. The next place is the synagogue in which Christ read the scriptures, and made that remarkable address which so offended his countrymen that they led him to the brow of the hill, to cast him down headlong. The synagogue is sixty by twenty-five feet, a mean and filthy place. Walking about the streets we saw what we saw at Tiberias — men knitting stockings, and women grooming the horses, lugging water-jars, and doing the heavy work. That same Nazareth would be a paradise for some men I know of.

Our camp lies near the fountain of the Virgin. The spring derives its name from the tradition that the angel first appeared to Mary when she was drawing water at this fountain. Probably she used to come here, as this is the common source from whence the people obtain their spring water. We went out each evening and saw the women come down with the great water-jars on their heads, and go singing away with their load.

By a detour we made a visit to Safet, said to stand higher than any other town in Palestine. We spent one night there. I found the place have a brighter, fresher, and more pleasant look than any

SPRING AT NAZARETH.

other I saw in Palestine, probably because many of the houses have been erected within a few years. In 1837, an earthquake occurred which shook the whole mountain and threw down a large part of the

THE CARPENTER'S SHOP.

place. A large number perished, among whom were four thousand Jews. The signs of the earthquake will be found all about. The old houses are found to have seams and cracks in them. The earth also shows seams and rents that were made in its rocky bosom on that day of wrath.

At evening we ventured into a Jewish synagogue. A large number of men were reading the scriptures. We took off our hats, but they flew at us and made us put them on again, and then they went on with their reading in a dull monotonous tone, swaying the body forward and backward as they read. The Jews are very numerous, and formerly had a printing-press and a book establishment. The Jews all through Palestine are a wretched-looking class of people. They wear a black hat, like a bean pot, and a long robe trimmed with cheap fur, and have a long curl of hair hanging down in front of each ear. Some one says that "a company of Jews look like the tenants of a hospital suddenly turned out by fire, and clothed in whatever came first to hand."

RIP VAN WINKLE.

IN SAMARIA.

VALLEY OF SHECHEM.

"We set our faces toward Jerusalem to-day," said the master, on Monday morning, as he stood in front of his tent in Nazareth.

"Yes, Jerusalem!" answered one of his friends.

"How mournfully you speak that word — Jerusalem."

"I cannot help it."

"Are the associations sad?"

"Very."

"Now, to me it is otherwise."

"To most persons it is. But I never can think of that city without a sigh."

"But why?"

"Because it was the scene of our Lord's death, and seems to be enveloped in a cloud of woe."

"I have been looking forward to the time when I should see Jerusalem, as one of the most tender moments of my life."

"You will doubtless find it so; for you have accustomed yourself to the idea."

"Yes, but we have something to see before we get to that city."

What the master saw before he reached Jerusalem, he tells the boys in this letter.

SAMARIA.

The great plain of Esdraelon stretches from Nazareth to Samaria. Our Sunday was spent in the former place, and it was a day of peculiar quiet and pleasure. We have three Sabbaths every week. Friday is the Mohammedan Sabbath, and the Moslems do not like to work on that day. Then Saturday is the Jewish Sabbath, and among Jews secular operations are generally suspended on that day; while the first day of the week being our Sabbath, we refused to travel or make purchases, — so we had three Sundays in one week.

On Monday morning, the camp was broken up before the sun arose; and when the king of day came forth from his bedchamber in the east the party were capering over the vast plain of Esdraelon. This plain, extending from Jenin to Nazareth, is eighteen miles long and fifteen miles wide, and is fertile enough to supply grain for all Palestine. It is the old battle-ground of Palestine. Almost every foot of its soil has been saturated with blood, and is distinguished for some scene of heroic daring. This was the famous Megiddo, where a battle occurred between Necho, king of Egypt, and Josiah, king of Judah, in which the latter was wounded by an arrow, and put into his chariot to be driven to Jerusalem, where he soon died.

Here on this plain, Barak and Deborah gained their great victory over Sisera. Barak was encamped on Mount Tabor with ten thousand men, and when Sisera came upon this plain, he came down and slaughtered his whole army. Sisera met with a sad fate, for after his great defeat and the slaughter of his army, a woman named Jael went out to meet him as he fled, and invited him to her tent. He entered, and being very tired, went to sleep after taking some refreshments; and as he slept on the earth, Jael took a nail, and with a hammer pounded it through his temples and nailed him to the earth. By and by, Barak came along in full pursuit after Sisera, and Jael took him into

PLAIN OF ESDRAELON.

her tent and showed him the dead captain, with his head nailed to the ground.

In riding across this plain, we pass the village of Jezreel, where Ahab and Jezebel, to get Naboth's vineyard, had him executed for blasphemy; El Fûleh, or "the Bean," where Gideon gained his battle with the men who lapped the water; Endor, where the witch lived whom Saul consulted; Nain, at the gates of which the young man was raised to life; Shunem, where lived the Shunamite woman, and several other places of much historic interest.

It was on this plain that Kleber, one of the bravest of Napoleon's generals, fought what is called in military annals, "the battle of Tabor," in 1799. For six hours he resisted with three thousand French troops a disciplined Turkish army of thirty thousand, one half of whom were the famous Mameluke cavalry. "Kleber," says the historian, "had left Nazareth with all his troops, in order to make an attack on the Turkish camp, but he was anticipated by the enemy, who advanced to meet him with fifteen thousand cavalry, and as many infantry, as far as the village of Fûleh. Kleber instantly drew up his little army in squares, with the artillery at the angles; and the formation was hardly completed when the immense mass came thundering down, threatening to trample their handful of enemies under their horses' hoofs. The steady aim and rolling fire of the French veterans brought down the foremost of the assailants, and soon formed a rampart of dead bodies of men and horses; behind this they bravely maintained the unequal combat for six hours, until at length Napoleon, with the cavalry and fresh divisions, arrived on the heights which overlooked the field of battle, and, amidst the multitudes with which it was covered, distinguished his men by the regular volleys which issued from their ranks. He instantly formed his plan. General Letourcq was dispatched with the cavalry and two pieces of artillery against the Mamelukes, who were in reserve near Jenin. With the remainder he attacked the enemy on the two flanks and rear, while Kleber assumed the offensive in front. The Turks, thus exposed to a concentric fire, fled in utter disorder; and hundreds were mown down by the grape-shot, as they floundered through the marshy plain."

Crossing Esdraelon the view is magnificent. The plain is wide, dotted with villages and Arab tents. Here on this plain we have a fine view of old hoary Hermon. Wherever we go in this country this splendid mountain is in view, its pale blue cone rising to the clouds, covered by its eternal snows. "Sheik of Mountains," Prime calls this lofty elevation, and royally it rises above the hills, to an altitude of ten thousand feet or more above the level of the sea, its triple peak surrounded by a blue haze, and its central pinnacle, with its white nightcap on, is a more commanding spectacle than any other mountain in Syria. Well is it called "Jebel-esh-sheik,"—Monarch of Mountains. Though miles away, the rarity of the atmosphere made it appear near at hand,—the snow on its crown and breast flashing in the sun seemed its kingly robe of diamonds, and it became the magnetic object on which the eye gazed often and reverently.

With this mountain in view, we reached the valley of Nablous, at the entrance of which is Jacob's Well, an object of the greatest interest to every Christian. There is something to see, but much more to think about at this point. I will try to describe the location of the well. Imagine two bold but beautiful mountains rising before you. Between them slopes a beautiful valley, miles in length, far up which you see the ancient town of Shechem. The vale is traversed by caravans, and various evidences of life are seen, as you gaze about its extended length. The mountains are Gerizim and Ebal. Gerizim is the Mount of Blessing, and Ebal the Mount of Cursing. Moses named these mountains and designated their uses. Before his death he referred to this spot in the following language: " And it shall come to pass, when the Lord thy God hath brought thee in unto the land whither thou goest to possess it, that thou shalt put the blessing upon Mount Gerizim, and the curse upon Mount Ebal. Are they not on the other side of Jordan, by the way where the sun goeth down, in the land of the Canaanites, which dwell in the champaign over-against Gilgal, beside the plains of Moreh?"

From the entrance of the people into the country, these mountains were connected with blessing and cursing, one looked upon with affection, and the other with terror. I can scarcely conceive of a

NABLOUS.

landscape view more beautiful than that which is present before us; the mountains on each side, the long herds, caravans, and watercourses, and Shechem, with its shining towers and glittering minarets

JACOB'S WELL.

in the distance. On a low spur of Mount Gerizim is Jacob's Well, at the mouth of which Christ sat talking with the woman of Samaria. Norman McLeod, in his beautiful essay, says that "the well is not what we understand by that name. It is not a spring of water bubbling up from the earth, nor is it reached by an excavation. It is a shaft cut in the living rock, about nine feet in diameter, and now upwards of seventy feet deep. As an immense quantity of rubbish has fallen into it, the original depth must have been much greater, probably twice what it is now. It was, therefore, intended by the first engineer as a reservoir rather than as a means of reaching a spring. Then, again, if any wall, as some suppose, once surrounded its mouth, on which the traveller could rest, it is now gone. The mouth is funnel-shaped, and its sides are formed by the rubbish of old buildings, a church having once been erected over it. But we can descend this funnel and enter a cave, as it were, a few feet below the surface, which is the remains of a small dome that once covered the mouth. Descending a few feet, we perceive in the floor an aperture partly covered by a flat stone, and leaving sufficient space through which we can look into darkness."

I judge from the appearance of the well at the present time, that Jacob dug away the earth until he came to the ledge of rock. Then he made his excavation. When the shaft had been sunk he built over the place a vaulted chamber, about ten feet square, and at the top of the vault laid the stone of opening. Then the earth was levelled over the vault up to the stone. On this stone Christ sat when he talked to the woman. Christ was on his way to the North. His course lay along the valley in which this well was found. The city of Shechem, then in its glory, was some distance from the main street, and when the travelling Messiah came to the well, instead of going into the city, he sent his disciples to procure food while he rested on the stone. While they were gone the woman came. Long and tedious was the distance which she had come with her waterpot upon her head, and in the heat of the day and weariness of the work, she desired to be told how she might avoid coming again to draw.

It is a tender spot to visit. It is authentic, and so intimately connected with one of the most touching scenes in the life of the Son of Man that it is associated in all Christian minds with Olivet, Gethsemane, and Calvary. We sat down on the stone, read the narrative from the New Testament, while a Samaritan priest, understanding English, listened with the greatest attention, and responded frequently. After the reading he gave us many interesting legends and traditions of the place. The well we measured, and found it to be sixty-nine feet deep. Every year it is fully filled up with stones and rubbish. Around the mouth are broken fragments of a church erected over the spot about the beginning of the fourth century, which is referred to by Eusebius, described by Jerome, and destroyed during the crusades.

The vale of Shechem is full of water, " musical with streams," as McLeod says, and many have questioned as to why Jacob should have built a well here in a region of running waters. Porter, who spent so much time in, and wrote so much about the Holy Land, tells us that "the very same question we might ask in every section of the plain of Damascus. Nowhere in Syria are running waters more abundant, and nowhere in Syria are wells more common. One acquainted with the East understands the mystery in a moment. Water is here the most precious of all commodities. Land is almost useless without it. It may serve for pasture; but the flocks that roam over it must have water. The soil may be fertile; but the fertility can only be fully developed by irrigation. Every proprietor, therefore, wishes to have a fountain or well of his own. A stream may run past or even through his field, and yet he dare not touch a drop of it. Jacob bought a field here; doubtless a section of the rich plain at the mouth of the valley; but this gave him no title to the water of the neighboring fountains. He therefore dug a well for himself in his own field; and indeed the field may have been bought chiefly with a view to the digging of a well. Every attentive reader of the Bible will observe that the patriarchs in wandering through Canaan had no difficulty about pasture; their herds and flocks were numerous, but the land was

SAMARITAN PRIEST.

wide, the inhabitants few, and the pasture was more than enough for all. But they had often serious difficulties and quarrels about water. The natives would not share their scanty supply with strangers, and they were thus compelled to dig wells for themselves; often at the risk of losing them. This is the case still in many parts of Syria. The pastures are free because they are plenty; the little wells and fountains are jealously guarded because they are few. In the Haurân, for instance, the vast flocks of the Bedawin are permitted to crop at will the rich pastures of Bashan; but the brave Druses will not let them near one of their little springs or reservoirs. Such was the origin of Jacob's Well."

Near by the well is the tomb of Joseph, the son of the patriarch. When he died he foresaw that the time would come when the Hebrews would go out of Egypt. He was aware of the promises made to Abraham, and could not endure the idea that when his father's family were reigning in the land of their salvation, his bones should lie amid the mounds and pyramids of pagan Egypt. So he commanded that his bones should go with the tribes to their home in the land of promise. They were not unmindful of this request, but when they went out of Egypt they took his bones, and in all that weary journey of forty years bore them up and down, never left them anywhere until they arrived in the Holy Land. And where could they put them — in what place so properly as in the soil watered by the well which his patriarchal father had made for himself and his family. The tomb is covered with a little wely, or chapel, unimposing and unattractive in appearance.

Evening had come, and turning our horses from this interesting locality, we drove up the vale to Nablous, a town built on the site and taking the place of Shechem. On our right was Mount Ebal, — the Mount of Cursing; on the left was Mount Gerizim, — Mount of Blessing. The former is a bold rugged mountain, that seems to frown upon every one that wanders along its base. Its top is crowned with cient ruins, and some have pretended to find there the remains of an altar built by Joshua. Mount Gerizim seems to smile in every changing feature. There is an irresistible fascination about it, and the gaze of the traveller always turns to it with pleasure. On its summit the Samaritans celebrate the Passover, and they claim that here, and not on Mount Moriah, Abraham came to offer Isaac.

We approach the city of Nablous, a place of eight thousand inhabitants. The streets are narrow, many of them arched, and the buildings have the appearance of great antiquity. We rode the whole length of the town. The people came out and scowled on us as we went by, and uttered all kinds of insulting epithets. There are a few Jews in the place, but Samaritans prevail largely, and the latter vie with the former in the hatred of Christians. We encamped in a grove of olives, some of them a thousand years old. We were surrounded all night by troops of dogs, and several times were obliged to go out and drive them away. We had some apprehension of an attack. We knew the character of the people, and were well on our guard. But no disturbance occurred, and we got through the night without any noteworthy incident.

The sun was hardly up before we stole away very quietly, fearing a shower of stones or of more deadly missiles, avoiding the usual way of egress from the city.

A ride of two hours brings us to Sebustia, the ancient city of Samaria, which in its day must have been one of the most magnificent of cities. In the "centre of a basin five miles in diameter, runs a flattish, oval-shaped hill to the extent of three hundred feet." On this hill the city of Samaria was built. The mound is terraced to its top, and rows of pillars, some of which still remain, show that the whole hill was formerly covered with elegant and elaborately wrought edifices. There are now about sixty houses and four hundred and fifty inhabitants in the village. The only building of any note is the church of St. John, built by the crusaders, to cover, it is said, the spot where John the Baptist was entombed after his martyrdom. The sepulchre is a little chamber excavated in the rock, and is gained by a descent of twenty-one steps. There is a tradition that John was beheaded here, and Jerome adopts it as a fact, and in the fifth century it was universally accepted. But Josephus says that John was beheaded in the Castle of Macherus, on the east side of the Dead Sea, and I do not know as the statement was contradicted until the fourth century. You may remember that in Micah there is a fearful prediction concerning this city. "I will make Samaria as an heap of the field, and as the planting of a vineyard; and I will pour down the stones thereof into the valley, and I will discover the foundations thereof." This terrible threat has been literally fulfilled. The very foundations of the city have been torn up, the pillars and capitals of the beautiful colonnades have been pitched over into the valley, and the whole place is literally " a heap." The entire hill is a mound of ruins. The village is almost inaccessible. Our horses panted as they clambered over the stones, or leaped the fallen pillars. The rude inhabitants were mostly absent, but enough remained at home to come out and stone us, and one or two of the company were obliged to draw their revolvers and drive them back. It was mournful to stand on this hill and look around upon the solitary columns rising here and there, so many mementoes of the past, — mementoes of a city which has had a large place in history — a city founded by Omri on this mound, which he bought for two talents of silver, about nine hundred pounds sterling; here Ahab built an altar to Baal; here Elijah and Elisha largely figured, and here, in the infancy of the church, Philip preached and gathered a congregation, to which Simon the Sorcerer belonged. We drove out of town amid the curses of the boys and women, down the rocky declivity, through the valley, by ruined villages, and picturesque ruins, until we reached the village Jeba, where, in a vineyard of vines and an orchard of figs, we lay down under the trees and slept for an hour. The ride from Jeba

EVENING ON THE HOUSETOP.

was one of great interest, through a fertile country, over beautiful meadows, by fine old ruins, passing Jenin where much attention was shown us. We also saw the site of ancient Shiloh, famed in Bible history for the exploit of the Benjamites, whose wives had been destroyed, and who determined to make good their loss by stealing an equal number of the most beautiful women of Shiloh, and making them their wives. When the bereaved six hundred returned to their forsaken homes they had no women, which was a most serious misfortune in the rebuilding of their towns, and the repeopling of their villages. So they remembered that the people of Shiloh had an ancient feast, which was celebrated just outside of their city. At such times the daughters of Shiloh came out to dance in the vineyards. In those times men and women did not dance together, and so the men remained behind. On this occasion, these Benjamites went and hid in the vineyards, and when the girls of Shiloh came out to dance they sprang up, and caught one each, and hurried back to their town of Gibeah. We do not read that any stir was made about the abduction of the damsels. Their friends probably thought they might as well get married that way as any other, and made no effort to get them back again.

Rip Van Winkle.

IN JERUSALEM.

TEMPLE AREA AND MOUNT OF OLIVES.

THERE was a great time among the boys when the letter of Rip Van Winkle from Jerusalem was received. More than the usual number of outside friends were invited into the meeting of the Triangle, and various services were performed before the letter was read. Among other things, the president called on Hal for a "declamation," and tne lad recited the following poem: —

> " Not from Jerusalem alone
> To Heaven the path ascends ;
> As near, as sure, as straight the way
> That leads to the celestial day
> From farthest realms extends ;
> Frigid or torrid zone.

"What matters how or when we start?
   One is the crown to all;
      One is the hard but glorious race,
      Whatever be our starting-place;
   Rings round the earth the call
   That says, Arise, depart!

"From the balm-breathing, sun-loved isles
   Of the bright Southern sea,
      From the dead North's cloud-shadowed pole,
      We gather to one gladsome goal —
   One common home in thee,
   City of sun and smiles!

"The cold rough billow hinders none,
   Nor helps the calm fair main;
      The brown rock of Norwegian gloom,
      The verdure of Tahitian gloom,
      The sands of Misraim's plain,
   Or peaks of Lebanon.

"As from the green lands of the vine,
   So from the snow-wastes pale
      We find the ever open road
      To the dear city of our God;
   From Russian steppe, or Burman vale,
   Or terraced Palestine.

"Not from Jerusalem alone
   The Church ascends to God;
      Strangers of every tongue and clime,
      Pilgrims of every land and time,
   Throng the well-trodden road
   That leads up to the throne."

After the recitation, and a song about Jerusalem, the letter of the master was opened and read.

JERUSALEM.

The round red Syrian sun was yet high in the heavens when our little cavalcade passed over the hills and approached the city of Jerusalem. Eager indeed were the expectations of the little company, and each one was striving to be the first to catch in the distance some outline of the place. At length we reached the summit of a hill, from which we could obtain a view of the city — the city of David, the city of Jesus, the city of God. There it lay full before us, an object of untold and indescribable interest. It was one of the happiest moments of my life. The trials and dangers of the way were forgotten; the cold shiver gave way to a thrill of exultation. Every pulse bounded, every nerve was keenly alive. There across the valley was Jerusalem, — its walls, its towers, its Zion, its Moriah, its Calvary. We were on one of the spurs of Gihon, the valley at our feet. Never before did I realize the force of the words of the psalmist, "Beautiful for situation, the joy of the whole earth is Mount Zion, on the sides of the North, the city of the great king." Never could I say before, with such enthusiasm and such emotion, "Peace be within thy walls, and prosperity within thy palaces." Longingly and lovingly we looked over to the sacred city, shouting, "Our feet shall stand within thy gates, O Jerusalem." And as we stood there, gazing over, the sun came out, the clouds rolled away, and Jerusalem lay blazing in the splendor of the closing day.

After viewing the city for a time, and reading several passages of scripture, and allowing our feelings to have their tender sacred flow, we rode to our tents, which were pitched in an olive vineyard outside of the city, not far from the Jaffa gate.

Let me give you a description of the camp. Our party, which was small at first, had increased to ten. To accommodate these persons we had one fine marquee, and three smaller tents. Five of us occupied the larger tent, and the others were accommodated in two of the smaller tents, while the other was devoted to the use of the cook. We had five iron camp bedsteads, with plenty of clothing. On pitching the tents in any place, a large carpet was spread on the ground and the table placed upon it, if pleasant, in the open air, if unpleasant, in the marquee. A table service of silver made the board look well, while our food was of the best kind, consisting of meats and fowl of all kinds, vegetables and fruit in great profusion. Our attendants consisted of our dragoman; our cook,—and a better could not be found in Europe; and Hallile, a Nubian, pretty as a girl, black as a coal, and smiling as May day. He was the man-of-all-work, and waited upon us at the table. Besides these we had several muleteers, who took

STREET IN JERUSALEM.

care of the mules and horses. Twenty-five animals, and nearly as many men, made up the caravan. At night, the mules and horses would be tied about the camp, and the muleteers would sleep around them for protection. Any party attacking the camp would be obliged to arouse the muleteers, who were our picket guard. Whatever tent life might have been to our brave soldiers on the Potomac, it was certainly very pleasant to us in Palestine. However, we did not sleep in our camp that night. The tents were wet, and ourselves chilled by the long ride through the storm, so we repaired to a Latin convent just inside the walls, where we remained that night.

And now we are at Jerusalem! But what can we do with it in the limits of a single letter? It is a city which might well demand a volume rather than the communication of an hour. To make myself as intelligible as possible to you, I propose, before describing the city itself, to notice its environs. Let us walk about Zion, and mark the towers thereof.

We started on Saturday morning, the Jewish sabbath, to walk around Jerusalem, outside the walls. It was a beautiful day, and Nature was in all the loveliness of the season. Leaving our camp, we moved down into the valley of Gihon, by the Upper Pool, over Fuller's Field, to the Lower Pool. The latter is now a cultivated garden, and fig-trees are growing in it. In the time of Christ it was a vast reservoir to supply the city with water. Leaving the pools, we soon struck the remains of the old aqueducts made by Solomon to introduce water from Bethlehem into his capital. These works show the immense expense of furnishing water to the city, and indicate an elaboration of means to make this supply which is truly wonderful to us. Moving slowly along the south of the place, we struck the Valley of Hinnom. This is a deep ravine, separating the city from the Mount of Offence and the Hill of Evil Counsel. It has a most unenviable notoriety. It comes to our notice in the first book of Kings as the place where Solomon, in his apostacy, set up an image of Moloch and made the people bow down and worship, for which crime the kingdom of Israel revolted from his house and family. From that time it was a place of idolatry. Ahaz and Manasseh there made their children to " pass through the fire," and led their people to practice abominable wickedness. At the end of the valley is Tophet, where infants were sacrificed to Moloch, and some have supposed that its very name was derived from certain coarse instruments of wire used there to draw the corpses of the poor victims as they passed through the fire to the idol. Josiah changed the character of the place from the worship of idols to a scene of pollution, making the valley the cesspool of the city, throwing in filth and burying the dead bodies of lepers that had been cast into it. The Jews and early Christians used the place to represent the state of eternal punishment. Across the valley of Hinnom is the " Hill of Evil Counsel." It is so called because the house of Caiaphas was located upon it, and there the wicked Jews assembled to take counsel against the blessed Saviour. The hill rises about five hundred feet above the valley below, and its top contains the ruins of an old convent, which dates back to the time of the crusades.

Near here is the famous or infamous Aceldama, or "Field of Blood," a deep cavern, or series of caverns, still used for burial purposes. It is on the southern slope of the valley of Hinnom. It is a place of bones and skulls. It was bought of a potter with the thirty pieces of silver which Judas received for the betrayal of Christ. A look down into the dens of death made us wish to leave the place and hurry away. All the waters in the Pool of Hezekiah would not wash out its stains.

Soon we came upon the Mou.t of Offence, or Mount of Corruption, Mount of Scandal as it is sometimes called. Here Solomon gave himself up to idol worship, and here offended a holy God, who will not tolerate idolatry. As long as this hill stands it will be a solemn remonstrance against the offence which that wise king committed.

Walking on, we struck a little rill which arrested attention. This was a stream of water from the Pool of Siloam, in the Tyropean valley. Following up the rill we soon came to the pool, which receives its waters from the "Fountain of the Virgin," at a little distance. There are several reasons why this charming water should be called the "Fountain of the Virgin." One tradition states that the Virgin Mary was accustomed to resort to this place for the purposes of purification, and hence in time it took its name from her. Another tradition, vouched for by Mejr-ed-Din, states that the water was known formerly as the Fountain of the Accused Woman, and it was deemed a test for women accused of great sin. If the person was innocent, she would drink without harm, and wonderful beauty was the result. But if she was guilty, she died, ere the sun set, of a most horrid, loathsome disease. When the Virgin Mary was accused of

POOL OF HEZEKIAH.

crime she was brought here, subjected to the ordeal, drank the water harmlessly, and ever after was gifted with a wonderful purity of expression, and secured the reputation among all her countrywomen of a saint.

The chief peculiarity of the fountain is its intermittent character. Whence its waters come, and why their flow should be intermittent, is only a matter of conjecture. They rush "furiously like a mountain torrent for twenty or thirty minutes, then intermitting for an hour or two, and in dry weather for a day or two." The Arabs account for this peculiarity by saying that an amphibious animal has charge of the waters, and their theory is that this dragon lives within the fountain. If he is awake, the water does not flow; but when he sleeps and cannot control it, it bubbles up. But men of science attribute the phenomenon to "the natural action of a syphon-shaped reservoir in the heart of the mountain." I am thus minute in the description of this fountain because it supplies Siloam, which is an oblong tank or reservoir, fifty-four feet in length, eighteen feet wide, and twenty feet deep. The remains of the porticos, which were once very beautiful structures, sheltering the multitudes who came to use the waters, are still seen. The pool was once probably covered with a roof, and in its day was elaborate and elegant. The fact that Siloam receives its waters from the Fountain of the Virgin, which I believe to be identical with ancient Bethesda, gives to it its name Siloam — signifying "sent."

Striking off from the objects on which we have commented, we enter the Valley of Jehosaphat, — "God judgeth," — which divides Jerusalem from the Mount of Olives, on the east. The brook Kedron flows through the valley, sometimes a tiny stream and sometimes a rushing torrent. We are soon among the ancient tombs — the tomb of St. James, a chamber excavated in the cliff, with its covered doorway, its elegant porch, and its sepulchral openings; the tomb of Zachariah, who was stoned in the reign of Joash, a monolith, solid in

IN JERUSALEM.

its contents, and beautifully ornamented from its rubbish-covered base to its pyramidal summit; the tomb of Jehosaphat, in which, a few years since, was found a Hebrew manuscript of the Pentateuch, the cloisters of which are now nearly filled with filth and rubbish; the tomb of Absalom, twenty-two feet square and fifty feet high, which has been filled with stones cast on it by the Jews, who spit upon it and curse it in memory of Absalom's ingratitude and treason. And many other ancient tombs there are, all worth seeing, and each of which has a history, but we must pass them by for want of space in this letter.

Still keeping on through the valley of Jehosaphat, we come to that sacred spot — the Garden of Gethsemane. In the time of Christ, the Garden of Gethsemane covered the whole base of Olivet; but a lot about three hundred feet square has been enclosed, to preserve the trees and to afford a retreat for devout strangers. Within the wall is

TOMB OF ABSALOM.

a walk around the garden, which is enclosed with a pale-fence. There are eight olive-trees in the garden, indicating a great age; and flowers and vines abound. The Latins have the charge of the place, and strangers are admitted for backsheesh. We went to the gate and were admitted by a monk, and stood on the very spot where Christ fell down, sweating great drops of blood. A clergyman of our party read the scripture narrative of the terrible agony which Christ endured in that place, and then we all knelt on the ground in prayer. It was awful to pray in that place. There came rushing on us the particulars of that scene, which no pen has yet attempted to describe.

It was one of the sweetest and most tender hours in my life. I closed my eyes, and soon my senses were all asleep to the world around me. I had gone back eighteen hundred years. I was in sad Gethsemane. I heard the groaning Lord as he lay upon the ground. I caught the memory of that tremendous agony. I saw the blood-sweat fall to the ground. I saw the angels as they came to strengthen him. And when I opened my eyes again it seemed as if my soul had received a shock, a jar, as when one is suddenly, roughly awakened from a charming dream.

Walking rapidly back to our tents completed the circuit of Jerusalem. We had seen the walls, passed the various gates, beheld the people as they went in and out, and had a fine idea of the surroundings of the city of God.

We are now prepared to enter the gates and see the interior of Jerusalem. There is generally a feeling of disappointment on the part of those who visit the city, and we felt it. We went in one morning, entering at the Jaffa gate. On each side of the gate outside was a long line of lepers,—men, women, and children,—their bodies in the various stages of decomposition. Their emaciated hands were held out for charity, and piteous indeed was the spectacle which they presented. Formerly this class of persons was driven away to the Lazar city, but they are now allowed to sit at the entrances of the city, begging of all who go in or out.

The streets within the place are narrow, irregular, crooked, and untidy. The houses are generally mean, low, and gloomy looking. The people, with a few exceptions, indicate poverty and sorrow, and the stranger, as he travels from one object of interest to another, cannot fail to see that God has marked with his divine curse the city where His son was neglected and crucified.

The city is elevated above all the surrounding region, being twenty-two hundred feet above the level of the sea. But beyond the valleys rise the mountains, which seem to guard the city. On the

MOSQUE OF OMAR.

east is the triple-topped Mount of Olives, its terraced sides rising steeply from the Valley of Jehosaphat. On the south is the so-called Hill of Evil Counsel, overhanging the wild ravine of Hinnom. On the west, the ground ascends by rocky acclivities to the brow of Wady Beit Hanîna. On the north is the hill of Scopus, a western projection of the ridge of Olivet. Around the city runs a wall, sufficient for the purpose for which it was erected, but entirely unfit to stand a discharge of artillery. The circumference of the walls is but twelve thousand nine hundred and seventy-eight feet,— four thousand three hundred and twenty-six yards,— or about two and a half miles. These walls are pierced by five gates,— the Joppa Gate, the Damascus Gate, the St. Stephen's Gate, the Dung Gate, the Zion Gate. Besides these gates, which are now in use, are two others that have long been closed,— the Gate of Flowers and the Golden Gate. The shops of the city are mean and filthy, the houses wretched and uncomely, and the whole appearance of the place is that of barbarous desolation. The present population is about sixteen thousand; of whom six thousand are Jews, six thousand Moslems, two thousand Greeks, and two thousand are made up of other sects.

The first building within the gates is the tower of Hippicus, of which Josephus tells us that "it was built by Herod the Great, and named after a friend who had fallen in battle. The form is quadrangular, twenty-five cubits on each side, and built up entirely solid to the height of thirty cubits. Over this solid part was a large cistern, and still higher were chambers for the guards, surmounted by battlements. The stones in its walls were of enormous magnitude,— twenty cubits long, by ten broad, and five high. Its situation, too, was commanding; for it stood on a rocky crest which rose from the summit of Zion to a height of fifty cubits." Of one of the towers which still stands, the others being in a crumbling condition, Porter remarks that "the lower part is built of huge bevelled stones, measuring from nine to thirteen feet in length, and some of them more than four feet high; the upper part is modern, and does not differ in appearance or workmanship from the other towers. The height of the antique part above the present level of the fosse is forty feet. It is entirely solid, and recent excavations have shown that for some height above the foundation it is formed of the natural rock, hewn into shape or faced with stones."

Leaving the tower behind, you strike into Via Dolorosa, the long, narrow street which led out from the judgment-hall of Pilate, through which Christ passed on his way to execution. The monks have invested almost every step in this street with interest, for they have attached some legend to almost every foot of it. The first object of interest in the street is the "Church of the Flagellation," where it is said that Christ was beaten with rods. Still further on is an arch spanning the way, Ecce Homo, where it is said that the cowardly Roman governor brought forth the Redeemer and showed him to the people, saying, "Behold the man." Then we reach a place where, as Christ passed along, he leaned against a house for protection, leaving the impression of his shoulder in the wall. There is pointed out another spot, where Christ met his mother, and held with her a tender and last interview. Next we come to the house of Dives; and there are Greek priests who will show you the very stone on which sat Lazarus, covered with sores, begging for bread. Just the place where Christ fainted under the cross comes next, and where it was taken from his shoulders and laid upon Simon the Cyrenean. Then you will be shown the place where, after he had recovered, he turned on the weeping women of Israel, saying, "Weep not for me, but for yourselves and your children." And there, too, is the house from which Veronica came forth, and wiped the gory face of Christ with the handkerchief, which is now preserved with great reverence and care at Rome.

Via Dolorosa conducts to the Church of the Holy Sepulchre, one of the chief attractions of Jerusalem. It was commenced in 1048,

CHURCH OF THE HOLY SEPULCHRE.

and was never finished until 1810. It is supposed to stand over the spot where Christ was crucified and buried. It is a tasteless Romanesque edifice, and in itself of no interest. The fact that it stands on Calvary gives it its importance.

And here allow me to say that there is some dispute as to where Calvary is. Some say here, and others point out locations elsewhere. The traditionary account of the exact spot where the cross stood is said to be this: The Empress Helena, mother of Constantine, was directed by God to search for the true cross, the spot where it stood, and the tomb of the Saviour. At the age of seventy-nine she entered on her mission. The pagans had buried the cross, and built a heathen temple on the spot where it stood on the day of crucifixion. But the empress went to her holy work, at length found the crosses, but for a time could not distinguish which was the one on which Christ died. At length they were submitted to a test. They were taken to a Christian woman who was dying in Jerusalem. The first and second were presented to her without effect, but when the third came it restored her to instant health.

It may be asked, what are the evidences that the place selected is the real Calvary. Dr. Robinson says it is not. Others, as careful and as able, say it is. Certain it is, that as early as the year 326 this site had been selected. The Apostle John, who witnessed the crucifixion, or knew all the facts pertaining to it, lived nearly seventy years afterward, and many others who were present at the tragedy, must have carried the knowledge of the place forward nearly a century; so that it seems to me that it would have been impossible for Constantine or his empress mother to have made any mistake. The knowledge of the exact spot must have been transmitted from the thousands who saw the deed committed to their children and grandchildren; and had the emperor fixed upon a site a mile or two miles from the place where the event transpired, a thousand voices would have been heard stating the traditions which had been handed down to them. The early Church could hardly have failed to know all about this great transaction, on which so much was depending. They must often have referred to the place where the Lord was put to death, and the spot must have been as familiar to them as the Garden of Gethsemane or Mount Zion. It can hardly be supposed that from the death of John to the time of Constantine the spot where the Lord was put to death for the world could have been forgotten. Nor do we know of anything in the scriptural representation, the topographical argument, and the historical account which may not be reconciled with known or existing facts. Without, however, expressing a definite opinion, where men who have spent so much time in Jerusalem and who have given the subject so much attention differ widely, let us conclude that we are near the mount of martyrdom, and the sepulchre of the Son of Man. Eusebius was born in the year 264, only about one hundred and sixty-four years from the death of the Apostle John, and he adopted the commonly accepted sacred localities without a question or a doubt as to their identity. He was present at the dedication of the Martyron erected by Constantine, and delivered a discourse, and must have been familiar with all the steps taken by the emperor and his gifted mother in their investigations.

Various things are shown in the Church of the Sepulchre, — the Stone of Unction, on which the body of the Saviour was laid while being anointed for burial; the spot where his mother stood during that process, indicated in the floor by a colored marble, an iron cage, lighted by an ever-burning lamp, covering the spot; the stone on which the angel sat when he had rolled it away from the door of the sepulchre; the stony, sepulchral slab on which Christ rested three days while the tomb held him; the vault itself where the King of kings wrestled with the King of Terrors. Then, in a little chapel we find a fragment of the pillar to which Christ was bound when he was scourged. Pilgrims touch the pillar with a rod, and then kiss the rod. Then comes the prison where Jesus was confined before his death, and the mount itself — Calvary, which is crowned with marbles, which are laid open so that the places where the three crosses are said to have been set in the rock, are seen.

STONE OF UNCTION.

All these places are near together, and one comes away with a confused and mixed idea of the whole thing. And yet here, doubtless, Christ was crucified! Here he was laid in the sepulchre! Here he rose from the dead! It would be mockery to attempt to tell how one feels when reaching down and touching with his hand the cold, wet earth, where it is supposed the cross stood. The very ground seems damp with blood. The rock seems to tremble yet as if it felt the shiver of the earthquake which shook it eighteen hundred years ago! It would be mockery to attempt any description of the emotions which surge over you as you crowd into the sepulchre, about seven feet square, and on your bended knees bow your head down upon the stony couch, and weep in memory of him who once reposed there in death, remembering that in this little cell Christ had his last conflict, here trampled death beneath his feet!

Another day in Jerusalem is given to the Temple,—alas, the temple of God no longer! At early dawn we left our camp to see the pavements and broken stones of what was once the finest edifice on the globe. As the Bible student knows, the first edifice was planned by God, the materials gathered by David, and the foundation laid by Solomon, B.C. 1011, on the threshing-floor of Ornan the Jebusite, on the summit of Mount Moriah. For seven years the workmen labored upon it, but no sound of the hammer was heard during all that period.

The building was all framed together, part fitted to part, before being brought here. For four hundred and twenty years the structure stood, the wonder of the world, when it was destroyed by Nebuchadnezzar, king of Babylon. The second Temple was built by Zerubbabel, B.C. 534, on the ruins of the first, but without much of the former glory. Antiochus Epiphanes polluted it, and set up the image of Jupiter Olympus on its grand altar. Judas Maccabæus purified and repaired it; but time and war wasted it again, until the time of Herod the Great, who repaired it with great magnificence. The structure covered the whole top of Mount Moriah, which had been walled up all around so as to give ample space. The structure stood until after the crucifixion, and was at length destroyed by Titus, by a singular coincidence, or rather a striking providence, on the same day of the same month that the first Temple was destroyed by the Chaldeans.

When the Turks came into possession of the holy city, they built upon the old foundations of the Temple the Mosque of Omar. It costs five dollars to each person as an entrance fee, and we were obliged to wander about the premises with our shoes off, and as it had rained the night before, and the water stood in puddles upon the worn and broken pavements, the exercise was by no means agreeable.

Would you understand how the Temple area appears at the present time? Imagine a hilltop levelled down, and the sides walled up, forming an area or square of about six hundred feet on each side. A wall, thick and massive, rises round it, while it is paved within with large, flat stones, which are moss-grown, broken, and defaced. In the centre of this area, where once stood the Temple, stands the Mosque of Omar, an octagonal building, each face of which is sixty-six feet. The edifice is one hundred and seventy-five feet high, surmounted by an elaborate and elegant dome. The interior is very imposing and beautiful, though the interiors of all the mosques are cheerless on account of their want of furniture.

The most conspicuous object in the mosque is the Sakhrah, or sacred rock. It seems that when the flinty top of Mount Moriah was graded down, this rock, some fifty by forty feet in dimensions and ten feet high, was left in its natural state, with no marks of the chisel upon it. The traditionary account was that on this rock Abraham built the altar on which his son Isaac was laid; that on it David offered his sacrifices before the Temple was erected; and that afterward it became the grand altar of the Jewish nation. The Mohammedans think that from this rock their great prophet ascended to Paradise. They even say that the mark of his foot is still upon it, though they do not often show it.

There is not much remaining of the old Jewish Temple. These

ST. STEPHEN'S GATE.

time-beaten paths, the foundations, and some subterranean passages are all that are left. The word of God is fulfilled. The prediction of Christ was verified. All that stood above the ground at the time the Redeemer lived was tumbled down — not one stone being left upon another.

No Jew is allowed to enter the Temple area, but there is a place in the Tyropean Valley where the western foundation of the earliest house of God is exposed to view. To this place the Hebrews come every Friday to moan and wail. The sight is a very touching one. From one hundred to five hundred Jews assemble, and as they read the Lamentations of Jeremiah they swing backward and forward, bow and wail; and then go again and again to kiss the stones. So long have they done this, and so passionate have been their kisses, that for a considerable distance the coarse, rough stones have been smoothed and polished by the lips of these devotees. I read from my Bible while the Jews read from theirs, and then went with them and kissed the stones, thinking of Him who saw the Temple and predicted its destruction, who now is the light and glory of the heavenly temple.

The question has often been asked, "What has become of the sacred vessels, and the immense wealth of Jerusalem?" It can hardly be supposed that God would allow all the sacred vessels to be forever ruined, and the general impression has been that the Jews, when the Roman armies came upon them, hid the Ark of the Covenant, the holy things of the Temple, and much that pertained to Jewish worship, and at some time, when God is ready, they will be found and be brought forth, to the joy and wonder of the ages. They are probably somewhere beneath the Temple, or some of the public edifices, and when the archæologists get at work they will bring them up. Dr. Barclay, who has written well on Jerusalem, and whose acquaintance we were fortunate enough to make at Jaffa, says that, "It is a very general belief that amongst the spoils of the Temple carried to Rome by Titus were the identical candlestick, golden altar and table, the silver trumpets, etc., that had been provided by Solomon; but this is a great mistake. Such of this furniture as was brought back from Babylon by the Jews on returning from captivity was carried to Antioch by Antiochus Epiphanes, when he despoiled

Jerusalem, and emptied the Temple of its secret treasures and left nothing at all remaining.' The sacred trophies carried away by Titus were those with which the Holy House was furnished by Judas Maccabeus on purifying the Temple after its profanation and desertion. On reaching Rome, the golden vesels and other sacred implements were deposited in the temple of Concord; and although some of them may have fallen a prey to the devouring element when that temple was destroyed, A. D. 191, yet history distinctly informs us that they fell into the hands of Alaric, when he sacked the city, A. D. 410. And about half a century afterwards most or all of them appear to have been carried to Carthage by Genseric, king of the Vandals, when the city fell into his ruthless hands, but seem to have been returned to Rome, or at least recovered by the Romans, after the victory of Belisarius. There appear to be reliable notices of them both at Ravenna and at Constantinople afterwards; and tradition, at least, reports that they were finally restored to Jerusalem by the Emperor Justinian, and it is supposed by many that they still lie concealed in some of the secret subterranean recesses of the Temple Mount."

There is one picture to be painted before we leave our subject and close our present letter. We must go out and view the Mount of Olives, "over against the Temple." American travellers generally go out on Sabbath afternoon, and cross Mount Olivet, as far as Bethany. And no walk on earth can be more suggestive of pious thoughts. It is the walk that Christ used to take when he sojourned on earth. Over the mountain, in a little town that nestled close to the brow of the hill, lived some of his friends. Here dwelt Lazarus, whom he raised from the dead, and Mary who sat at his feet, and Martha who loved to entertain him at her hospitable board. For this family, Christ seemed to entertain a special fondness. He loved their society, and often when weary went over the hill to take his evening meal in their ever-cheerful home.

I went out one Sabbath afternoon. The Jews in the city were all busy, for their holy day had passed, but outside all was still. Only the song of the bird, and the hum of the insects, and the rustling of the grain, disturbed the silence. I went down into the valley of Jehosaphat, through the bed of Kedron, to the base of Olivet, and struck into the very road which we suppose Christ took when he went out to visit his friends. Passing by the Garden of Gethsemane, I was soon ascending the hill. But here pause in the way while I describe the Mount of Olives. Sit down on the ground by the wayside, or rest on the stones, while I make your minds familiar with this hill which we are ascending.

Olivet is on the east of Jerusalem, and separated from it by the brook Kedron. It is not a Mount Washington, towering to the clouds, and covered with its crown of snow, nor even a Monadnoc, lofty in its verdant pride. It is a respectable hill, or a ridge of hills, rather than one solitary mount, only one hundred and seventy-five feet above the city, and but half a mile from it. On the centre hill is the little village of Tur, which has one tapering minaret, and beneath that minaret is the Church of the Ascension, built, it is supposed, on the spot from which our Lord went up to glory. The hill is sparsely covered with olive-trees, and streaked with roads and foot-paths leading over or winding around it.

We reach the summit, and ascending to the gallery of the minaret look off upon Jerusalem spread out before the eye. "We look down," says an eyewitness, "the shelving side of Olivet into the dark, bare glen of the Kedron, sweeping from the distance on the right away down to the left. The eye follows it till it is joined by another dark ravine, coming in from behind a high ridge to the westward. That ravine is Hinnom, and that ridge Zion. On the left bank of the Kedron we can just observe through the olive-trees the white pointed top of Absalom's pillar, and the flat gravestones of the Jewish cemetery, and farther to the left the gray excavated cliffs and houses of Siloam. In the foreground beyond the ravine is the beautiful enclosure of the Haram — the octagonal mosque with its noble dome in the centre, occupying the site of Ornan's threshing-floor and

JERUSALEM AND THE MOUNT OF OLIVES.

Solomon's Temple; the flagged platform around it; and then a grassy area with its olives and cypresses encircling the whole. At the left-hand extremity is the mosque el-Aksa, easily distinguished by its peaked roofs and dome — formerly the church of St. Mary. Beside the enclosure at the right-hand corner is a prominent group of buildings, with a tall minaret adjoining them. This is the pasha's residence, and the site of the Fortress of Antonia. The massive ancient masonry at the southern angle of the wall is very conspicuous; and so likewise is the double-arched gateway in the side, generally known as the 'Golden Gate,' now walled up. Farther to the right, north of the Haram area, is St. Stephen's Gate, and the white path winding up to it from the bottom of the Kedron at the Garden of Gethsemane. Northward of the gate, along the brow of the valley, runs the city wall, formidable-looking in the distance with its square towers. To the right of the Haram, a broad irregular ridge extends northward, thinly inhabited, interspersed with gardens, and crowned by a mosque and minaret. This is Bezetha. The low ridge of Ophel is on the opposite side of the Haram, sinking down rapidly into the bed of the Kedron behind Siloam; it contains no buildings, but is thickly sprinkled with olives. It can now be seen how these three hills, Bezetha, Moriah, and Ophel, form one long ridge. Behind them is a valley, dividing the city from north to south, and falling into the Kedron just above its junction with Hinnom."

Turning from the view toward Jerusalem, we look out in the other direction. "Here we stand," says the same observer, "on the very brow of the mount. The 'Wilderness of Judea' commences at our feet, shelves down in a succession of naked white hills and dreary gray glens for ten miles or more, and then dips abruptly into the deep valley of the Jordan. A scene of sterner desolation could not be imagined. The Jordan valley comes from the distance on the north, gradually expanding into a white plain, and terminating at the Dead Sea, a section of whose waters is seen over the lower cliffs of the 'Wilderness.' The winding course of the Jordan can be traced for some distance up the plain, by its dark line of verdure. Away beyond this long valley rises suddenly a long unbroken mountain-range, like a huge wall, stretching north and south far as the eye can follow it. The section on the right is within the territory of Moab; that in the centre, directly opposite us, was possessed by the Ammonites; while that on the left hand was anciently called Gilead, and still retains its name. Evening is the proper time for this view, for then the pale blue lights and purple shadows on the Moab mountains are exquisitely beautiful. The glare too of the white wilderness is subdued; and the deep valley below appears still deeper from being thrown into shade."

We cross over the mountain, and reach Bethany, on the hillside. Here lived the family that Jesus loved. The house in which they once abode is pointed out, and the tomb of Lazarus is also shown, but the identity of both is very doubtful. Returning, we reach the summit, pass around the Church of Ascension, and descend by a different road from that we took in coming up. A sudden turn in the road brings the city to our view. Until now it had been hidden. As it bursts upon us we stop, and in wonder and amazement gaze out upon it.

We remember a scene that once transpired here. Christ was crossing the Mount, and a great multitude of people were with him. They wanted to take him to the city and crown him as their king. They shouted, "Hosannah, hosannah to the Son of David." But as Christ turned this point in the road, and the city burst upon him, he stood still and wept — wept that Jerusalem knew not her day. Singular and precious were my thoughts that Sabbath evening as I sat in the door of my tent, looking on Jerusalem on one side and on Olivet on the other.

Did space allow we might dwell long in describing the scenes in and about the city; the walls and the gates, the Castle of Antonia, the room where the Lord's Supper is supposed to have been instituted, the fountains and pools, the tombs and monuments, but our space is exhausted, and I must stop writing. Many are never permitted to see the earthly Jerusalem. Few people are so situated that they can travel so far, even to see the place where the Lord was crucified.

> "Jerusalem — far distant land —
> Our longing feet can never stand
> Upon those far-off hills.
> We know these deep and yearning thoughts
> To see those consecrated spots,
> Can never be fulfilled.
>
> "Yet day by day our feet draw near
> A land that to our soul is dear —
> The New Jerusalem;
> Its gates of pearl, its golden wall,
> God's glory shining o'er it all,
> The Lamb the light thereof.
>
> "And oft on wings of earnest prayer,
> Our soul draws near that land so fair,
> And views its Heavenly Home;;
> And as we gaze towards Zion's hill,
> Its fair foundations glisten still,
> With minaret and dome.
>
> "Sometimes our souls in saddened hours
> Feel the soft touch of friends of ours,
> Who long since went to dust;
> Then, dim and undefined, it seems
> Like the soft rays of sunset gleams,
> That land comes down to us.
>
> "Not over ocean's heaviest breast,
> Or toilsome days of dark unrest,
> Shall we that city see;
> But soft we pass through quiet death,
> With calm repose and fleeting breath —
> Jerusalem, to thee."

Yes, that upper Jerusalem we may visit, within its walls we may dwell, all its joys we may share. Jerusalem the golden! In old Jerusalem Christ was mocked and denied. In the new Jerusalem he is honored and worshipped. In old Jerusalem he was crowned with thorns. In new Jerusalem he is crowned with glory. In old Jerusalem he was crucified. In new Jerusalem he is enthroned. Jerusalem the golden!

RIP VAN WINKLE.

IN JERICHO.

ELISHA'S FOUNTAIN.

EARLY one morning, Rip Van Winkle was aroused by one of his friends, who came to the door of the tent, shouting, —
"Professor! Professor!"
"What is it?"
"Why, get up and see, good friend."
"It is not time to get up yet."
"Yes, it is; and you are wanted."
"What for?"
"The party are out in the valley holding a council of war."
"Is the enemy in sight?"
"No."
"Then what is it?"
"The subject of a visit to Jericho, the Jordan, the Dead Sea, and the South, is contemplated, and the matter is being discussed."

"Well, let them discuss."

"But they want you."

"What for?"

"They say that it will not do to decide until the professor is present."

"But I am only an *attaché* of the party. They do not want me to help decide."

"But they do. They say your opinion is worth all the rest."

"Well, I will come along as soon as I can get ready."

"So do, for you know how fully they all rely upon your judgment."

"Just six minutes and ten seconds and I will be there."

"All right."

In less than the time mentioned, Rip Van Winkle was seen in the midst of the group of men who were debating their plans. As they saw him come, one of them said, —

"Professor Van Wert, we have been thinking of going to the Dead Sea, making an examination thereabouts, and returning to this place again. We want your opinion."

Rip Van Winkle heard their plans and approved of them, and said he would like to go with the rest. Though the gentlemen had been strangers to him until within the few weeks that they had been together, he had become much attached to them, and they felt a deep interest in him. What they did, and where they went, we will let the traveller tell in his own way.

JERICHO.

My last letter was written when I was sitting at the door of my tent, looking off upon Jerusalem. You will now see that our quarters have been changed, and we are on our way to the Dead Sea. Though the whole land is stagnant, and marked with death, there is always something novel and strange drawing attention which gives variety even to that God-cursed region. In one place the remains of a city wherein some of Christ's marvellous works were done, meets your eye, reminding you of transactions which will never be forgotten nor repeated. Then you will remember that the next piece of desert through which you ride has become historic on account of some world-famed battle which has been fought or some dreadful tragedy which has been enacted there. Then you leap some tiny

ARAB AT TENT DOOR.

brook or streamlet scant which has a sacredness which all the ages cannot take away. The whole life of Christ, the founding of the Christian religion, the most remarkable events, the most wonderful histories ever known, are crowded into a little country not larger than the state of Vermont, and though stagnation reigns, yet each new step is marked with something to which the traveller turns, and on which he gazes with ever-kindling enthusiasm.

We started one morning on a tour toward the south. We wanted a flag, and because we could do no better, made one that morning before we started. We could not purchase one. There was none for sale in Jerusalem, so we carefully prepared the cloth, and, with needle and thread, we all sat down and sewed the stripes together. As we sat there with our work on our knees, we formed a very much more respectable "sewing circle" than we often see at home, where the ladies don't sew, but come just at tea time, for the good supper, and then go home thinking they have been at the "*sewing circle*." There was not room enough on our flag for the whole number of stars, so we put on the original thirteen. Just as we had finished it, a regiment of Turkish soldiers marched by, and we hung out our banner, proud there, before Jerusalem, that we lived under the stars and stripes.

At ten in the morning our tents were all down and packed safely on the backs of the mules, and we were leaving Jerusalem behind us. The trip being somewhat dangerous, a mounted guard had been furnished us by the pasha, a sort of irregular soldiery kept for the purpose of escorting travellers through regions infested with bandits and robbers. Sweeping with our long train over the Mount of Olives, through the town of Bethany, we were now going down to Jericho. I never before realized the force of the expression, "going down to Jericho." From Jerusalem it is down hill all the way, and the roads are villainous in the extreme. The whole course is eminently suggestive. Through dark, solitary ravines, by the mouth of yawning caverns, looking out of which the swarthy Bedouins could be seen, and sometimes their long pointing guns, over rocky declivities, leaping our horses where they could neither trot nor walk, we pursued our way for several hours. You notice that I say "hours." The distances are measured by hours, not by miles. If you ask, "how far to such a place?" the answer is "so many hours." A man may be an hour going five miles, or he may be two hours going one mile. Some

ARABS IN PLAIN OF JERICHO.

days, we were riding hard to make five or six miles. The road to Jericho is of this description. After leaving Bethany and passing a famous fountain covered with a Saracenic arch, close to which are the remains of an old *Khan*, the way becomes frightful. "Into a bleak glen, the road winds for an hour or more, and then, leaving it to the right, passes through a broken country of chalky hills till it reaches an extensive, ruined caravansary, situated on the top of a bleak ridge. Some broken walls and fragments of arches remain standing; but they are scarcely sufficient to afford us a shade while we rest a few minutes to draw water from the deep well. This is considered the most dangerous part of the road; and somewhere near it Sir Frederick Henniker was stripped, wounded, and left for dead by the Bedouins in 1820. He was probably thinking of the parable of the Samaritan when the assassin stroke laid him low. I venture to state that no one will advance much beyond this place without at least feeling how admirably fitted the region is for deeds of violence and blood; especially if he gets a sight of some of the half-naked Arabs who are generally found skulking amid the ruins, or perching on the rocks around. On passing the ruin we enter a region still wilder than that we have left behind. Dr. Olin says of it, that 'the mountains seem to have been loosened from their foundations and rent to pieces by some terrible convulsion, and then left to be scathed by the burning rays of the sun.'"

Through such a wild desolate country we rode until nearly night, when we struck the Plain of Jericho. The Arab escort suddenly paused, and bade the company halt, and called to one of the party who was in advance of the rest, to return. Two or three of them then rode forward, and scoured the plain, riding up and down among the gaps to be sure that no Bedouins were lurking there to start up as we approached, for robbery and murder. A few days before we crossed this plain, two or three of our countrymen were robbed of all they had, their horses taken away, and they left to get back to Jerusalem on foot. We fared better, being a much larger and more formidable company, and we were careful that the fellows should see that we were well armed. Indeed, if the Arabs judged us by the bold show we made of revolvers and pistols, they would conclude that we were the most desperate set of characters that ever rode over the plain, as ready to shoot a Bedouin as a squirrel.

At length Jericho appeared in sight, and what a sight! A pile of

RUINED AQUEDUCT, NEAR JERICHO.

ruined villages heaped up into one, looking more like a lot of brick-yards than a royal city, such as we expected to see. On the right of Mount Gilgal, where the twelve stones, which Joshua took out of the river Jordan when he crossed with the Hebrew hosts, were set up as a memorial, and where, also, the Tabernacle was pitched for the first time in the Holy land, we encamped. The site of Gilgal is near Jericho, but not a vestige of the place remains. It has been destroyed, plucked up by the roots and ploughed for the fruitful field. After our tents were all pitched, and dinner had been served, we walked over to see Jericho! There have been three Jerichos. The first was very ancient in its origin. It was the city of palm-trees, and must have been very beautiful in its time. This was the place that was taken by Joshua after being encompassed by the Israelites.

The second Jericho was built in the time of Ahab, by Hiel the Bethelite. It flourished exceedingly, and became a very noted place, but in time it was again destroyed. The third city was founded some time before Christ, and was in his day, a considerable place. It continued awhile to increase in wealth and power, but the hand of God was laid upon it, and it went to sad decay.

There was a terrible curse pronounced on the first Jericho, which was wonderfully verified in the building of the second. When Joshua had taken the place, he destroyed it by direction of the Almighty, and then pronounced a curse upon anybody who should endeavor to rebuild it, in the words: "Cursed be the man before the Lord, that riseth up and buildeth this city Jericho; he shall lay the foundation thereof in his first born, and in his youngest son shall he set up the gates of it." This was a most peculiar curse, but it was fulfilled. Five hundred years after Joshua destroyed the city, Hiel set himself about rebuilding it. He knew about the curse. But he lived in a wicked age, and was the servant of a very wicked king, and dared defy the Almighty. So he commenced the work, and the curse commenced with it. While the foundations were being laid, Abiram, Hiel's eldest son, was killed, and while the gates were being set, Segub, his youngest son, died, crushed, as is supposed, by falling masonry. The word of God tells it all in one graphic sentence,— "He laid the foundation thereof in Abiram, his first born, and set up the gates thereof in his youngest son, Segub!" And so may we learn were all God's curses and threatenings fulfilled.

Entering Jericho just before sundown, we found it to be a most forlorn and God-forsaken place. The children howled and yelled at us, and set dogs on us. The women followed us with scowling faces, and taunts, and we were glad to escape. On emerging on the other side of the town, we found the house in which Zaccheus is said to have lived at the time he entertained the Saviour. The tree into which he climbed is not standing, though it is almost a wonder that some one near by is not pointed out as the veritable tree from which he expected to get a good view of the illustrious personage. The house which is now occupied by a Turkish governor, is in a good state of preservation, and is the largest in or about the town.

At night we had an idea of life in Jericho. Between us and the city was a grove, and after dark, the people came out of their filthy houses and assembled here. It was a strange gathering. Some were cooking their evening meal, some were sporting on the green sward, some were dancing under the trees, some were sleeping, some in groups were singing their monotonous songs, and every conceivable thing was being practised, from the Moslem offering his prayers, to the most utterly indecent exhibitions, to which there seemed to be no restraint. I never knew, until that evening, how near human beings could come to the brutish creation, or how low immortal souls could descend. Until late in the evening they kept up their revel, and then the quiet of night hushed them in slumber.

While sitting in our tents this evening, our friend the dragoman came in and told us that women outside wished to speak to us. " *Women!* " we said. "Yes." We wondered what lady friends we had in Jericho! We could not conceive what women should want of us, and some of the gentlemen began to fancy that their wives, thinking it not well that they should have all the pleasure of the trip alone, had followed them across the ocean and overtaken us at Jericho. But Hallile, one of our attendants, told us that the women were the dancing girls of the country, who are accustomed to visit the camps of European travellers and give them an exhibition of their dancing skill. They go through their dance, for which the travellers are expected to pay something. I was not unwilling to have the exhibition, but some of the party objected, and we sent the servant out to send the girls away. The dancing girls of the East are an institution of themselves, and those who are acquainted with dancing in this country have little idea of the same art in oriental nations. I don't know but the dancing of the Arabs is as decent and as sensible as our own. Let me describe it in the language of another: — "Whenever a town is reconnoitred, in the poorest and shabbiest huts on the outskirts, the dancing girls have their homes. Different from all other females, their faces are never covered. Their dress is of a light rose color, a delicate yellow, or an equally soft blue — of the thinnest gauze. Their foreheads are covered with jewels of Turkish gold or silver coin, suspended in strings, one below another. They are stockingless, but wear red morocco shoes, stiff and hard. Their belts are strung with trinkets, such as small silver triangles, or little bells, and all have metallic cymbals in each hand. Stripping off their shoes when the music begins, their hips suddenly rise up, their bodies swing either way, their toes cramp into the sand or into the floor, while their countenances assume an earnestness of expression; the fervor increases, the features become impassioned, the cymbals click, and thus they pass from one degree of excitement to another till, quite exhausted with the intense action of every muscle in the frame, the exhibition closes." Why this disgusting contortion of the muscles of the body should be called dancing, I don't know. One needs to see it but once to remember it with a feeling of loathing and abhorrence.

Sunrise in the morning found us on the banks of the Jordan — at the spot where it is supposed Christ was baptized, a short distance from the entrance of the river into the Dead Sea. The Jordan is a sacred river, divided for the passage of the Children of Israel, and notable for the baptism of Christ. It has figured largely in the annals of the church. It rises far away in the north, at the roots of

Anti-Lebanon, and pours down over long inclined planes and twenty-seven rapids and cataracts for two hundred and ten miles, until it comes to the Dead Sea. It descends from the point where it rises to the Sea of Tiberias, which is six hundred and fifty feet below the

BANKS OF THE JORDAN.

Mediterranean. Through that sea which is thirteen miles long and six miles wide it rushes on its way scarcely mingling with its waters, and pouring out at the lower extremity, and descending again in swift torrents to the Dead Sea, which is one thousand three hundred and sixteen feet below the Mediteranean. Almost all the way, it flows through a deep sombre glen varying from two hundred to six hundred yards in width, and from forty to ninety feet below the level land above. The banks are of clay and mud, and shrubs and trees of various kinds grow on the shores. The stream itself varies in width and depth. At the place we visited it was, at the time, about one hundred feet wide and very deep, and the current was very swift. Travellers differ much in their descriptions of the depth and breadth of the Jordan, from the fact that they view it at different seasons of the year — one when the snows of Anti-Lebanon and the north of Syria have swollen it, and others when the summer suns have licked up the waters, so that they have nearly all disappeared. I saw the river at sunrise that day. It was wide and deep. Along its course trunks of trees, the roots of shrubs and many other fragments were rapidly borne along. There was water enough to drown a hundred thousand men, and it was not hard to recall that time when our Lord, beneath the shadow of the trees as they overhung the stream, was baptized in the Jordan.

Once a year a most singular scene is witnessed here at the Jordan. The Greek Christians of Palestine have an annual custom of coming in large numbers to bathe in these waters. It takes place in Passion Week. On Monday swarms of pilgrims come from all parts of Palestine and encamp at Gilgal. "The desolate plain," says one who has witnessed the thrilling scene, "is thus suddenly filled with life; and the stray traveller who witnesses the scene will be strikingly reminded of the multitudes that thronged, eighteen centuries ago, to the 'baptism of John.' Every Christian state of Europe and Asia has its representative there; and there, too, is seen, picturesquely grouped, every variety of costume. At their head marches the Turkish governor of Jerusalem, or his deputy, with an armed escort, to guard against the bandits, who, since the days of the 'Good Samaritan,' have infested this desert road. Some hours before dawn on the following morning a host of little *tom-toms* suddenly give forth their discordant but stirring roll, and a thousand torches suddenly flash amid the thickets of the plain. Over the desert presses the crowd in silence. A ruddy glow along the eastern horizon brings out into bold relief the summits of the Moab mountains, and gives a hint of the sun's approach; and the pilgrims, as they descend the steep bank from the upper terrace, now see, in the pale morning light, the dark line of foliage that hides the sacred stream. An opening in the fringed border is soon after discovered, and the motley throng hastily dismount, and, as Mr. Stanley graphically describes it, 'set to work to perform their bath; most on the open space, some farther up among the thickets, some plunging in naked, most, however, with white dresses, which they bring with them, and which, having been so used, are kept for their winding sheets. Most of the bathers keep within the shelter of the bank, where the water is about four feet in depth, though with a bottom of very deep mud. The Coptic pilgrims are curiously distinguished from the rest by the boldness with which they dart into the main current, striking the water after their fashion alternately with their two arms, and playing with the eddies, which hurry them down and across, as if they were in the cataracts of their own Nile. . . . A primitive domestic character pervades in a singular form the whole transaction. The families which have come on their single mule or camel now bathe together, with the utmost gravity; the father receiving from the mother the infant, which has been brought to receive the one immersion which will suffice for the rest of its life, and thus, by a curious economy of resources, save it from the expense and danger of a future pilgrimage in after years. In about two hours the shores are cleared; with the same quiet they remount their camels and horses; and before the noonday heat has set in, are again encamped on the upper plain of Jericho. . . . Once more they may be seen. At the dead of night the drum again awakes them for their homeward march. The torches again go before; behind follows the vast multitude, mounted, passing in profound silence over that silent plain — so silent that, but for the tinkling of the drum, its departure would hardly be perceptible. The troops stay on the ground to the end, to guard the rear; and when the last roll of the drum announces that the last soldier is gone, the whole plain returns again to its perfect solitude.'"

And speaking of the baptism of Christ, reminds us that John, his forerunner and harbinger, came clothed in "camel's hair," and "eating locusts and wild honey." The locusts of the East were an article of food, being prepared in different ways. Sometimes they were pounded up and mixed with flour and sometimes boiled, broiled or roasted. And yet it is a question whether John did really eat this food, or whether he lived on the sweet locust-pods, on which the prodigal fed, called in his case, the "*husks.*" It was an article generally used in feeding the swine. Certain is it that this was the food the prodigal son wanted, and which no man gave to him, and many suppose it was the food of John, called in this case "*locusts.*" The fruit is now used by the common people as an article of food. It has a sweetish smell, and is not at all unpleasant to the taste.

Well, here, boys, I must leave you. You can think of me encamped near the Jordan, from whence I shall go to a spot where I know you would like to be with me.

Rip Van Winkle.

IN BETHLEHEM.

OLD KHAN.

"Where do you suppose Rip Van Winkle will take us to-night?" asked Fred of his two fellows, on the day when the next budget was to be opened.

"I don't know," answered Charlie, "but I presume he will return from the Jordan to Jerusalem, and his letter will be from that city."

"I think not," said Will. "The master has plenty of time on his hands, and I do not think he will turn back so soon. He may go through the desert to Egypt, and if so we shall find him on the Nile. But we shall see when we meet to-night."

"Don't you sometimes peep into the letter before you open it in the Triangle?" asked an outsider who was by.

"On my honor, no!"

"I should think you would."

"We agreed some time since that the letters should be opened in public meeting, and shall hold to it."

"Shall I come to-night?"

"Yes, glad to have you."

"I know of several who will be present."

"Yes, we have invited twenty-five — as many as our parlor will accommodate."

"Then I will be there."

When the hour arrived a goodly company of gentlemen and ladies was present, and the Triangle opened in the usual way, and the letter was opened, and found to be dated at

BETHLEHEM.

I left you last week at the ford of the Jordan, where we cut walking sticks, and gathered flowers. A brisk trot on our poor horses brought us to the Dead Sea, a very memorable sheet of water, and one that you would like to bathe in. We met with no adventure on the way, though the region is infested with robbers who will attack any party that may not be strong enough to resist them. Not long before we were there, an Englishman in company with a clergyman from Philadelphia, with their two wives, took it into their heads to visit Jordan without an armed escort. They reached the river in safety, but in crossing over to the sea were met by bandits who robbed them of everything they had, taking every article of clothing they wore, and leaving them to get back to the city in the best way they could.

As one approaches the Dead Sea, he is conscious of a drowsiness which sobers and saddens him. It may be the emotions, or the deso-

HARVEST CARRYING IN PALESTINE.

lation of the surroundings, but few fail to feel it. The spirits go down, vivacity ceases, and a sadness comes over all the senses. The sea is called in Scripture, "the Salt Sea," the "Sea of the Plain," the "Sea of Arabah," and the "Sea of Sodom." It is forty-six miles long

CHURCH OF THE NATIVITY.

by ten and a half wide, an oblong pool containing about two hundred and fifty square miles area. As already remarked, it lies one thousand three hundred and sixteen feet below the Mediterranean Sea. It is very deep, measuring, only a mile from the northern end, over one thousand three hundred feet. The chief characteristics of the

EASTERN GLEANERS.

water are its weight and saltness. A gallon weighs about three pounds more than common water, and has in it over three pounds of saline matter, of which one pound is of common salt. Ordinary sea water contains only one-half pound of saline matter to the gallon.

It has been a common idea that a bird trying to fly across the sea would soon inhale the poisonous vapors and fall dead into the water. But this is not so. Birds do fly over the waters, though there is so little to attract them that they are not often seen about the sea. They keep away from it because there is nothing there for them to feed upon. Now and then a shrub is seen growing, but vegetation finds little to support it there. The shores of the north end are covered with black coal-like bituminous stones, which will burn if put into a hot fire. They resemble in appearance a slaty kind of coal.

A bath in the water is more novel than comfortable. A New York clergyman who went in says: "I cannot conceive worse torture than that plunge caused me. Every inch of my skin smarted and stung as if a thousand nettles had been whipped over it. My face was as if dipped in boiling oil, and the skin under my hair and beard was absolute fire; my eyes were balls of anguish, and my nostrils hot as the nostrils of Lucifer. I howled with pain; but I suspended when I heard my friend's voice. He had swallowed some of the water, and coughed it up into his nose and the tubes under his eyes. The effect was to overcome all pain elsewhere while that torture endured. It came near being a serious matter with him; and, as it was, his voice suffered for a week, his eyes and nose were inflamed as if with a severe cold, and the pain continued severe for several days. Recovering our feet with difficulty, we stood, pictures of despair, not able to open our eyes, and increasing the pain by every attempt we made to rub them with our wet hands or arms."

Our party were soon floundering about upon the water. It was quite amusing. Portly men would float upon the surface like a cork. Tall thin men would act like a pole — if one end was down, the other end was up. A little scratch or bruised spot upon the body would be the source of intense pain as soon as the water touched it. On coming out the skin is found covered with a saltish scurf that is quite unpleasant. Generally, travellers visit the Dead Sea first and wash off the salt in the Jordan afterward, but we had tried the Jordan first, and were to suffer the salting process all through that sultry burning day.

The shrubs growing on the shore of the lake are the *lotus* and the *osher* plant. The lotus is described by Lynch, as "having small darkgreen, oval-shaped, ivy-like leaves. Clustering thick and irregularly upon the crooked branches, are sharp thorns half an inch in length. The smaller branches are very pliant, which, in connection with the ivy-like appearance of the leaves, sustain the legend that of them was made the mock crown of the Redeemer. Its fruit, as I have before mentioned, is subacid, and of a pleasant flavor."

The osher plant bears what are called the apples of Sodom. These apples are about the size of a small lemon, filled with bitter juice, which when dried changes to ashes. Thus they are spoken of by Tacitus: "The herbage may spring up, and the trees may put forth their blossoms, they may even attain the usual appearance of maturity, but with this florid outside, all within turns black and moulders into dust." Josephus in his description of them says, "Which fruits have a color as if they were fit to be eaten; but if you pluck them with your hands, they dissolve into smoke and ashes."

About half way down the lake is the famous pillar of salt, known as "Lot's wife." For ages such a pillar is said to have been in existence, and now and then allusions have been made to it by travellers. Lynch, in his Dead Sea expedition, found it, as it had been described at Usdum: "Soon, to our astonishment," he says, "we saw on the eastern side of Usdum, one-third the distance from its north extreme, a lofty, round pillar, standing apparently detached from the general mass, at the head of a deep, narrow, and abrupt chasm. We immediately pulled in for the shore, and Dr. Anderson and I went up and examined it. The beach was a soft, slimy mud encrusted with salt, and, a short distance from the water, covered with saline fragments and flakes of bitumen. We found the pillar to be of solid salt, capped with carbonate of lime, cylindrical in front, and pyramidal behind. The upper or rounded part is about forty feet high, resting on a kind of oval pedestal, from forty feet to sixty feet above the level of the sea. It slightly decreases in size upwards, crumbles at the top, and is one entire mass of crystallization. A prop, or buttress, connects it with the mountain behind, and the whole is covered with *débris* of a light stone-color. Its peculiar shape is doubtless attributable to the action of the winter rains."

By some ill-fortune our dragoman when we returned from the Dead Sea left his skins containing water behind, and we were an hour on our way before the loss was discovered. At length when thirst began we inquired for drink, and found that we had none. This was a bad condition of things. We had several hours' ride before us. The sands of the scorching desert over which we rode were hot and blistering. The Syrian sun was pouring down its hottest beams, and the thermometer stood at one hundred degrees.

"How far is it before we come to water?" we asked of our dragoman.

"Half hour," was the reply.

We thought that we could stand that very well, though the salt sea had parched our lips, and terrible were our sensations. We rode on half an hour, and then inquired again, "Dragoman, how far is it to water?"

"Half hour," he replied.

Still on we rode another half hour, and again asked the same question, and received the same answer.

"You rascal," we replied, "you told us an hour ago that we

SHEPHERD BOY OF BETHLEHEM.

should come to water in half an hour—now tell us truly how far it is before we can get any water to drink."

Finding himself driven to the wall, the dragoman put spurs to his horse, saying, "Water is half hour — hour — hour and a half."

And this was the only reply we could get all that day.

"Do tell us, dragoman," we would say, "how long it will be before we reach some spring or well where we can find water," and the same unsatisfactory reply would be given, "Half hour — hour — hour and a half."

I never knew what thirst was before. I thought I had experienced it. I had read about it in books. I had heard of men left for days without water on the sun-heated deck of some ship, but I never knew the meaning of that word, thirst! Hour after hour we rode on in the scorching heat, brains throbbing, pulses beating, heads aching, and senses failing. At length in the middle of the afternoon we came to water. It was in a sort of excavation under a rock. The water had drained down from some recent rain, and was a foot or two deep. The top of it was covered with a green slime, and one or two dead owls were lying on the surface. That was the water we were to drink. Out of that cistern we were to obtain our supply. Under ordinary circumstances the idea of drinking such water as that would have been so revolting that we should have turned away in deep disgust. But not so then. We were thirsty. We knew the meaning of that word. So we lowered our tin cans down into the pool, and drawing up the thick, putrid liquid, swallowed it without compunction. And, certainly, no Cochituate, with Lake Wenham ice in it — no Croton, from crystal goblets, ever tasted so delicious as that stuff from that well in the desert. Only once that day did we get a glimpse of the Bedouin robbers of the wilderness. In the forenoon, a company of them saw our train moving along, and dashed across the plain to intercept us, but on coming near found that we were too strong for them, and with a few curses hurled harmlessly at our escort,

CONVENT OF MAR SABA.

they strapped their long guns over their shoulders and rode hastily away.

Late in the afternoon we reached the convent of Mar Saba, one of the most remarkable in the world. There we were to stop after our toilsome journey. On entering, the monks furnished us with lemonade, *arakee*, and other drinks, which we took according to our tastes and inclinations — some the harmless lemonade, and some the fiery arakee, an intoxicating liquor distilled from anise seeds, and other sweet herbs of the region. This convent is located in a ravine through which runs the brook Kedron, and is said to be the most " extraordinary building in Palestine." The convent was founded by St. Sabas in the year 483. It is partly natural, being hewn in the cliffs, and partly artificial, chambers having been built out, and projecting over the valley below. Imagine a deep ravine, with a high ledge of rocks, or series of bluffs, rising precipitously from it, and these rocks excavated, pillared, chambered, and fortified, so that it seems as if the very precipice itself was one vast edifice, and you have some conception of this convent. It is wildly picturesque, and is a study for the curious traveller. After supper we went in through these queer chambers which are used by the monks for various purposes. They did not put us into cells at night, but provided for us in the large dining-room of the convent. The most remarkable room we saw there was the charnel-house, in which they keep the monks after they are dead. For a year, we were told they are allowed to lie in their monkish habits, and then their bones are cleaned and they are housed away in this hideous chamber. We saw one or two monks, embalmed as we suppose, spending their probationary year in their robes, waiting for its expiration, to be taken to pieces and fixed out for a final disposal. The history of the founding of the convent is this: " St. Sabas, the founder of the convent, is said to have been born in the year A. D. 439. He was a man of extraordinary sanctity; and assuredly no stronger proof could be given of the high veneration in which he was held than the fact, if fact it be, that he drew thousands of followers after him to this dreary region. Some writers affirm that as many as fourteen thousand swarmed to this glen and its neighborhood during the saint's life. Sabas was a native of Cappadocia, but at a very early age he devoted himself to conventual life, and went to Palestine. After visiting many parts of the country in search of a home, he withdrew to this spot about the year 483, and began to form a religious community. He soon afterwards founded the convent, which still bears his name. He subsequently received from the Patriarch of Jerusalem the appointment of archimandrite, or abbot of all the anchorites of Palestine. In the controversy raised about the Monophysite heresy, which so troubled the Church during the early part of the sixth century, he took a leading part; and on one occasion, with a little army of monks, he marched to Jerusalem, drove the emissaries of the heretical Patriarch of Antioch from the city, though accompanied by imperial troops, and pronounced anathemas against him, and all those of his communion, in the presence of the emperor." The saint died — for saints will die, in 532, after which, for twelve centuries, his holy home was a place of blood, sometimes being held by one faction, and sometimes by another, until now, a peaceful community of monks inhabit it, and it is a hotel for travellers on their way from the Dead Sea to Bethlehem. A story is told by the monks, and many believe it, that when the saint came here, he found one of the crevices in the rock which he supposed would make an admirable place for a recluse to live in poverty, retirement, and with God. But on climbing to it, he found a fierce lion to be a prior occupant. The saint told him his purpose; and the king of beasts, appreciating his pious wish, left the premises, and for years brought the hermit his food day by day, and at night slept at his door as a faithful sentinel. Several ages have added to this place, so that now it is so extensive that no stranger could find his way through it.

BETHLEHEM, LOOKING EAST.

No lady is ever allowed within the gates of this strange edifice. Were a woman dying, she would not receive permission to enter. Sometimes in perilous times, however, when the country was so filled with robbers that it would be utterly unsafe to stay in camp outside, women have been hoisted from the outside to the top of the high tower, and thus allowed to remain over night. There is not much hospitality, nor much gallantry in this, but it is a way the monks have. When Mr. Prime was at this convent, he tried to take his wife in, but was not successful. "When the door at which we stood was opened," he says, "we found a lay brother there who was not booked up in the traditions. He politely invited us to enter. I asked him if Miriam could be admitted; and he said there was no objection. I waited a moment to send back to the tents for her; and he, in the mean time, stepped into the refectory to consult an older authority. When Miriam arrived, we advanced as far as the descent of the first steps, into the great court by the tomb of the saint, but there we were arrested by a cry that might have roused his bones, if the profane footsteps of a female had not already disturbed him. The father superior and a dozen brothers were begging Miriam to go out; and she paused a moment to enjoy their terror, and then retired to the gate, where a venerable monk soon joined her; and, making a thousand apologies, and relating the traditions to her great amusement, led her to the east tower, where she could look down into the convent, and where she was supplied with bon-bons, sweetmeats, jellies (and arakee!) *ad libitum,* while we entered the sacred precincts."

It is a wild and strange place, and as in the evening we wandered out, and looked up to the grotesque structure, we could not prevent imagination from investing each cell with nameless horrors and infernal tragedies. The valley of the Kedron, on the side of which the convent is built, or rather into the sides of which it is built, is about four hundred feet deep, and six hundred feet across from height to height; and the whole has been very appropriately styled a "city of caverns."

When morning came we were glad to gallop out the gates, and leave the dim, frightful old nest of caves behind us. A brisk ride of three and a half hours along the banks of the Kedron, across the dreary plateaus, brought us within sight of Bethlehem. As we rode toward the town we were reminded of the olden times. Shepherds were near, watching their flocks on the hills and in the valleys, as they did eighteen hundred years ago. The day was quiet, and all nature was hushed to calm repose. The words of Milton came to mind as we advanced, —

> " No war nor battle sound
> Was heard the world around ;
> No hostile chiefs to famous combat ran ;
> But peaceful was the night
> In which the prince of light,
> His reign of peace upon the earth began.
>
> The shepherds on the lawn,
> Before the point of dawn,
> In social circle sat : while all around,
> The gentle fleecy brood,
> That cropped the flowery food,
> Or slept, or sported on the verdant ground."

It seemed almost as if we should hear the angels sing, and we paused as we read the account of Messiah's birth — listening as we read to catch some seraph's anthem in the sky.

When near the town we met groups of young girls and children, old men and young men, coming out and going in, forming a beautiful and picturesque spectacle to the eye, and as the low wailing music fell on the ear, it seemed the sweetest place we had visited. You can hardly conceive of the beautiful effect of the whole scene, the costumes of the country corresponding so finely with the natural scenery, the whole effect heightened by the flowing robes and the showy colors.

Bethlehem! What sacred memories cluster around this place! The word signifies—" House of Bread," and the town is sacred in the annals of the people of God. Here Jacob buried Rachel; here Ruth came and gleaned in the fields of Boaz; here Jesse lived at the time David was anointed king; and here, greatest event of all,

WOMEN OF BETHLEHEM

the son of God commenced his earthly career, and the sacred majesty of heaven put on a robe of flesh.

Driving at once to the church and convent, we were in the midst of the sacred places. They are all under this church and convent edifice. The grotto of the Nativity, or the stable in which the Lord was born, has been recognized for seventeen centuries. It is beneath the church, which was erected by the Empress Helena in the year 328. The grotto, cave, or stable, as it formerly was, is a natural cavity in the rock, thirty-eight feet long by twelve in width, and is reached by crowded passages. Passing through these passages and entering the room, you find that the monks have marked every spot with an exactness which throws discredit on them all. There, under sixteen silver lamps, that are never allowed to go out, is a slab covering the exact spot, it is said, where the Virgin Mary gave birth to the son of man. Holding a candle down to the slab, you find a Latin inscription, which reads as follows: "*Hic de Virgine Maria Jesus Christus natus est.*" "Here Jesus Christ was born of the Virgin Mary." Near by is a stone trough, which is pointed out as the manger wherein the Lord was laid after his birth. Another spot is marked as the one where he was arrayed in swaddling bands. Though the exact spots are of course, uncertain, the cave is doubtless the one in which Christ was born. Indeed, writers who are skeptical on many of the places, give credence to this. Dr. Robinson says "The Cave of the Nativity, so called, at Bethlehem, has been pointed out as the place where Jesus was born, by a tradition which reaches back at least to the middle of the second century. At that time Justin Martyr speaks distinctly of the Saviour's birth, as having occurred in a grotto near Bethlehem. In the third century, Origen adduces it as a matter of public notoriety, so that even the heathen regarded it as the birthplace of him whom the Christians adored. Eusebius also mentions it several years before the journey of Helena, and the latter consecrated the spot by erecting over it a church."

Another subterranean cave is shown as the study of St. Jerome, where so many years of his toilsome life were spent, a fit place for a man to be alone and wrestle with God. An old portrait of the saint yet hangs in the room, which is dim and dreary enough for any recluse.

There is at Bethlehem what is called "The Milk Grotto." I should not omit a reference to that. "Tradition relates," says the historian, "that the Virgin and Child hid themselves here from the fury of Herod for some time before their flight to Egypt. The grotto is excavated in the chalky rock, which derives its whiteness, say the monks, from some drops of the Virgin's milk which accidentally fell upon it. Many are the pilgrimages made to this spot, and the reason is, the virtue attributed to the stone of miraculously increasing woman's milk. The stone is soft, and bits are broken off, and conveyed to every province of Europe, Asia, and Africa, in which Christian superstition has established its dominion, to be administered to such as need its wondrous efficacy. Even the Abbé Geramb bears testimony to its virtues. 'I shall make no remark,' he states, 'on the virtue of these stones or on its causes. I merely affirm, as an ascertained fact, that a great number of persons obtain from it the effect they anticipate.'" The few hours spent in Bethlehem are memorable ones. The quaint town, the attentive monks, the dim and dreary convent, the suggestive associations, all add interest to the day and the occasion.

From Bethlehem we rode to the extensive pools of Solomon, from which the king, in an aqueduct yet extant, carried water to the city of Jerusalem. Then on to the capital, which we reach at dusk, entering by the way of Olivet, taking the road which the Saviour took when they carried him over in triumph, and soon we were at our camp ground, under the branches of fig-trees, cooling ourselves in the door of our tents.

Before closing this long letter, which I will soon do, I wish to speak of a few things in general. I was afraid when I set out for the Holy Land that I should find things so different from what I had expected and imagined, that my feelings would be constantly shocked. But it was not so. Not only in Jerusalem, but throughout Palestine, I found things very much as I expected to find them, and indeed as I wanted to find them. The face of the country, the topography of the Holy Land, corresponded with my general idea; and the habits and customs of the people, so little changed from what they were centuries ago, seemed to bring up before me the narratives of that blessed Saviour, whose words are ever fresh and new. The hills looked us I thought they would look; the people dressed as I expected to see them; the cities, towns, and villages, were as I had heard them described.

The roads everywhere were dreadful. Indeed there were no roads worthy of the name, and I often wondered how our dragoman could take us through the country without being confused and losing his way. Sometimes the precipices were so steep that we were obliged to dismount and let our horses pick their way down as best they could, and again and again have I seen them roll over and over. At other times we pursued our way for miles over rough, ragged, rolling stones, that turned, and slid, and wabbled, and rolled as we trod on them, or as our horses put their feet into them. Sometimes the only way we could advance was to follow the bed of a stream, the water splashing on us as we rode along. I think there is only one decent carriage road from Mount Sinai to Mount Lebanon, and that has been built from Beyrout to Damascus, by the French government, That admits of heavy carriages, has been built at a great expense, and has required considerable time to complete it.

The climate we found much more favorable for our explorations than we had anticipated. Only one day — that on which we journeyed from the Dead Sea to Mar Saba — did the mercury in the thermometer rise higher than 100°, and on one occasion, at five o'clock in the morning, it was as low as 34½°, but generally ranging from 60° to 80°.

At almost every turn one is meeting something to remind him of Scripture, something to prove and illustrate the truth of the words of Christ and his apostles. The whole land is a sublime illustration of the truth of prophecy. The declarations of God are written, not only in the Bible, but they are burnt into the soil of Palestine. Jerusalem is the fulfilment of prophecy. Jericho, Capernaum, Tyre and Sidon, are fulfilments of prophecy. Everywhere the truth of God is seen in the history and condition of this land and people. Everywhere the truth of the Bible is seen in the destruction of cities and the wreck of once populous countries.

Rip Van Winkle.

IN HEBRON.

ABRAHAM'S OAK.

BEFORE leaving Bethlehem, the party with Rip Van Winkle at its head rode out gayly to visit a cave, famed in ancient history — the Cave of Adullam. It is about five miles from Bethlehem, and a ride of little over an hour brought the travellers to it. It is near the base of Jebel Furcidis and well answers to the description of the cave in which David hid. Dr. Thomson's description of his visit would answer for that of our party. "Having passed eastward of Tekoa, we descended a shallow wady for about a mile to some curious old buildings which overhang the tremendous gorge of Wady Urtas there called Khureitûn, which is also the name of the ruins. Leaving our horses in charge of wild Arabs, and taking one for a guide, we started for the cave, having a fearful gorge below, gigantic cliffs above, and a path winding along a shelf of rock, narrow enough to make the nervous among us shudder. At length, from a great rock hanging on the edge of this shelf, we sprang by a long leap into a low window which opened into the perpendicular face of the cliff. We were then within the hold of David, and, creeping half doubled through a narrow crevice for a few rods, we stood beneath the dark vault of the first grand chamber of this mysterious and oppressive

HEBRON.

cavern. Our whole collection of lights did little more than make the damp darkness visible. After groping about as long as we had time to spare, we returned to the light of day, fully convinced that, with David and his lion-hearted followers inside, all the strength of Israel under Saul could not have forced an entrance — would not have even attempted it. I see no reason to disturb the tradition which makes this the *hold* into which David retired with his father's house and his faithful followers when he fled from Gath. David, as a shepherd leading his flocks over these hills, was doubtless acquainted from his boyhood with all the intricacies of this fearful cavern, just as these Arab shepherds, his successors, now are, and what more natural, therefore, than that he should flee thither in the day of his extremity? It was out in the wild desert, far from the haunts of Saul, and not likely to be visited by him. It was also in the direction of Moab,

CAVE OF ADULLAM.

whither he sent his parents and the women of his train, while he abode still in the hold. Again, we know that many of his subsequent exploits and escapes from Saul were in this region and south of it; and, finally, there is a sort of verbal accuracy in speaking of the topography — David's family are said to have gone *down* to him from Bethlehem. Now this cavern is nearly two hours to the southeast of

HEBRON AND CAVE OF MACHPELAH.

that village, and the path *descends* rapidly nearly the entire distance. Let us therefore acquiesce in the tradition that this is the Adullam into which David fled fi om Gath, and in w iich he first collected and organized his band of trusty followers."

HEBRON.

It was early morning when the first view of Hebron, the old royal city of David, was first taken. It was an inspiring sight, and must have been magnificent when the place was in its former glory and splendor. Of course, within, like all the old cities of Palestine, there is an annoying disappointment, but approaching the city of Hebron from the northeast, a very fine view is obtained.

The objects to be seen in Hebron are the pools, the Cave of Machpelah, the manufactories of glass and filigree work—each on a small scale, to be sure—the mosque and a few other things. The city is reduced in population greatly from what it once was. It has now only seven thousand inhabitants, but these people are much more respectable and thrifty than those found in Jericho, Bethlehem, or Jerusalem.

Here, in the vineyards around Hebron, the spies sent out by Moses found the magnificent fruit which they carried back to show to the people as evidences of the fertility of the land. There is little now to suggest the grapes of Eshcol, or the vineyards of the earlier days. Waste, decay and desolation are written all around. And yet it is not hard to see what might be done here with proper cultivation. The natives make raisins of the grapes that are produced and send them to distant markets. The pomegranates also abound in this vicinity. Dr. Thompson speaks of this fruit, which was greatly esteemed. "There are several kinds of them," he says, "in this country. In Jebaah, on Lebanon, there is a variety perfectly black on the outside. The general color, however, is a dull green, inclining to yellow, and some even have a blush of red spread over a part of their surface. The outside rind is thin but tough, and the bitter juice of it

stains everything it touches with an undefined but indelible blue.
The average size is about that of the orange, but some of those from
Jaffa are as large as the egg of an ostrich. Within, the "grains" are
arranged in longitudinal compartments as compactly as corn on the
cob, and they closely resemble those of pale red corn, except that
they are nearly transparent and very beautiful. A dish filled with
these "grains" *shelled out* is a very handsome ornament on any table,
and the fruit is as sweet to the taste as it is pleasant to the eye. They

SOLOMON'S POOL.

are ripe about the middle of October, and remain in good condition
all winter. Suspended in the pantry, they are kept partially dried
through the whole year. The flower of the pomegranate is bell or
tulip shaped, and is of a beautiful orange-red, deepening into crimson
on some bushes. There is a kind very large and double, but this
)ears no fruit, and is cultivated merely for its brilliant blossoms, which
are put forth profusely during the summer."

The Cave of Machpelah is the wonder of the city. It is the

Westminster Abbey of Hebron. Here lie the bodies of Abraham, Isaac, and Jacob, with their wives Sarah, Rebecca, and Leah. What a company sleeping together in death! For ages no Jew nor Christian was allowed to enter the cave. Death would have been the penalty had any adventurous traveller dared descend into the dismal abode But in 1862 the Prince of Wales and his suite were allowed to enter, and others have since followed. If you care to read more than I have written, you can obtain various details in the work of Dean Stanley who accompanied the Prince of Wales, and who had facilities for obtaining information which have been granted to no other traveller since the days of the Hebrew kings.

RIP VAN WINKLE.

IN EGYPT.

THE Professor now leaves the land made sacred by the life, memories and death of the Saviour of mankind, and with his companions, journeys through the desert of Sinai, toward the dark coast of Egypt. He has been fortunate in finding so pleasant a party to travel with. The gentlemen composing it are men of culture, good habits, and rare conversational powers, and Rip Van Winkle finds himself a congenial spirit in their society. They agree to go to Egypt together, and so he can have the benefit of their company and kindness for many days to come.

The pleasure of a foreign tour depends very much upon the good temper and kindly spirit of those who travel together. Some parties split asunder, and the persons comprising them separate before half their tour is over. Want of congenial tastes, varieties in disposition and temper lead to this, and the party is broken up before it has had time for the various persons to become acquainted with each other. It was not so in this case, but every day cemented the friendship between the men who had fallen into company. Mr. Van Wert gives this account of his experience in Egypt.

CAIRO.

We have now reached the prominent Egyptian city. You may care to hear how we got here, and as it gives you some of my experience in camel riding, I may as well tell you about it.

At Hebron, we took camels and horses, and joined some other parties who were to proceed through the desert of Egypt. Persons who have never used these ships of the desert, as camels are called, know little about the sensations of those who take passage on them.

They soon become *seasick* on the dryest land, and get down from the hump with as much pleasure as a seasick boy lands from a yacht in New York harbor. To mount, to ride, and to dismount, are all awkward proceedings. But we get used to each process.

When we have passed the boundaries of Palestine, and are out upon the desert, the Arabs, who have been quiet and stolid in the towns and cities, seem to be in their native element, and give themselves up to hilarity and mirth. They have thrown off the incubus which civilization seems to put upon them, and are wild with joy. One day two or three of them came to us, as we rested for our lunch, and one said, —

"Gentlemans."

"Well, what is it?" inquired a gentleman whom we recognized as the unofficial leader of our caravan.

"Aboo and me wants — "

"What does 'Aboo and me' want?"

"To race."

FIRST RIDE ON A CAMEL.

"Well, scamper off as fast as your legs can carry you."
"We not wants to go on our legs."
"Whose legs do you want to go on?"
"Dromedaries' legs."
"What! a race with the 'ships of the desert'?"
"So you call him."
"Will there be fun in it?"
"Yes, much fun."
"Then go, and we will enjoy the fun."

Then commenced a race between those huge animals, driven to desperation by their drivers. We followed on, but they soon outstepped us, and in a little while became mere specks on the sand.

How we reached the Sinaitic region, spent a night at the Monastery of St. Catherine, and gave some days to hunting for the veritable mountain on which the Law was given to Moses, may not be of as much interest to you as it would to your older friends. I suppose you do not care much whether Jebel Musa, Jebel Serbal, or Mount Sufsâfeh is the real Sinai, and, so I will pass over all our interesting investigations in these localities, and take you at once to the land of the Nile.

We passed the wells of Moses, and the palm trees of Elim, and striking the Red Sea near where it is supposed the Children of Israel crossed, entered the town of Suez. There we stopped one or two days, left our camels and took more modern vehicles.

The town of Suez is a mean place, the streets narrow and unclean, the houses small and filthy, and everything about the neighborhood forbidding. Did not the exigencies of trade require the existence of the town, it would soon disappear. "The spot," says Dr. Randall, "from the very nature of the locality, seems destined as a resting-place for travellers. Situated upon the head waters of the sea — a place for embarkation whenever there is any traffic upon its waters — the gate of entrance to the great Sinaitic peninsula, and

THE RACE.

STREET IN SUEZ.

since the establishment of Mohammedanism, a rallying place for pilgrims upon the great caravan route from Grand Cairo to Mecca. There has been a settlement here in some form from time immemorial. Modern Suez, a few years ago a small, insignificant town, has, since the termination of the railroad here, rapidly increased in size and importance. It lies in about 30° of north latitude, and now contains some three thousand inhabitants. It is difficult to conceive of the barrenness and desolation that surrounds it. Washed upon

TOWN OF SUEZ.

one side by the waters of the sea, the barren wastes of desert encircle it upon the others. There is no fresh water within several miles of it, and then a very scanty supply. Most of the water used by the inhabitants, and all used by the engines, is brought from Cairo on the cars, and all the provisions are brought in from abroad. No green thing is seen in the vicinity, not a grass plat, not a tree or a shrub, to relieve the gloomy, sterile monotony of the place." To exchange camels, horses and donkeys for steam cars was a novel thing. In doing it we seemed to have leaped over the lapse of four thousand years, from the time of Abraham to our day. But despite the violence done to the romance of the thing, we were glad to do it.

The ride to Cairo was not marked with many incidents. At one of the stopping places, we had an opportunity of seeing the state railway carriage of the Khedive of Egypt, and a marvel of elegance it was. I have seen gorgeous state carriages of European monarchs, and splendid trains of cars on the railroads of our own country, but nothing like this. I did not imagine that I should find in the desert the most gorgeous train of cars that I ever beheld, but so it was. The locomotive was a most elaborate combination of gold, silver and steel. The cars were exquisitely finished and furnished, the upholstery being silver and crimson. The state carriages of France and England are dowdy and tasteless, compared with this specimen of oriental magnificence.

On examination of the locomotive I found that it was made in the United States, though I presume the decorations were put on in Egypt. At the time we discovered the fact that the locomotive was made in this country, a vast crowd was gazing at it. An enthusiastic countryman of ours was very proud that this gorgeous vehicle should be of American manufacture, so he pointed to the inscription, and significantly shouted, so as to be heard by hundreds of the gaping Egyptians, "Americana! Americana!" They answered with nods of affirmation. Then he pointed to himself and exclaimed, "Americana! Americana!" to indicate that he and the machine were both from the same country. With a shout the Egyptians responded, and the Yankee proudly retired. We thought there was something a little peculiar and suspicious in the shout, and asked our dragoman to tell us what idea the crowd had got from our friend. "They think he means," said the dragoman with a smile, "that he and the locomotive are both steam engines."

STREET IN CAIRO.

At every stopping-place along the way, we found large numbers of persons who had something to sell at prices fabulously low: roasted chickens, hot, plump and well-cooked for three pence each; eggs, well-boiled, four for a half penny; oranges, apricots, and other fruits, as much as one can carry away, for a trifle; bread, coffee, sandwiches, cake, lemonade and strong drink, that curse alike of Orient and Occident.

On the way the Nile is seen. The moment it comes in sight, the Arabs, who have seen it a hundred times before, crowd to the windows of the cars, and shout with pleasure, or gaze down upon its waters with silent delight. With an Egyptian the Nile is an object of great respect, if not of adoration. And well it may be so, for without it not a single human being could subsist in that arid, scorching region. It is rain and dew, food and drink, occupation and country, father and mother, to thousands who subsist upon its products.

On many accounts the Nile is the most wonderful river on the globe. It is not like your Mississippi, and your Ohio, and your Merrimac, ploughing on monotonously to the sea, bearing commerce like a dromedary, or turning water-wheels for millions of spindles like a slave. But from its unknown starting point, up in the land of mystery, it is full of romance, poetry, and fiction. Rising in a long undiscovered source, it comes down in two streams,—the White Nile and the Blue,—uniting near the city of Khartoom. On it rolls, washing the base of mighty pyramids, laving the shores of pathless deserts, traversing mighty deltas, and giving sustenance to a teeming population. In its flow it is charged with a rich mud, which in times of inundation it deposits as a vigorous fertilizer all over the land. It knows just when an overflow is needed, and at the given time, it breaks its channels, and wildly rushes over the plains, returning again when its beneficent work is done, and sweeping on majestically, pours itself into the bosom of the mighty sea.

We reached Cairo, the magnificent, about the middle of the afternoon, and repaired to the Hotel d'Orient, a sumptuous place, well worthy of the name it bears; and there being some time before night, concluded to take our first donkey ride. As a donkey ride is an Egyptian institution, just as much as the street-car is an American idea, I may as well describe it.

NILOMETER.

As we came down the grand staircase, and issued from the court, some fifty donkey-boys were standing in a line waiting for us, each holding a donkey by the bridle. I knew my great Master rode into

Jerusalem on such a beast, but for all that, could not help despising the ugly animal. His long ears before, and his wilful heels behind, his perverse habits, mulish disposition, treacherous eye, and grizzly back, were alike repulsive.

Then as I looked at the little creature, it seemed an act of cruelty for me to mount him, — I weighing two hundred pounds, and he about seventy-five pounds as I thought, apothecaries' weight! I was afraid I should break him down, his legs were so slender, and his bones so small. I seriously queried whether in justice I should not shoulder the donkey and give him the ride. But the boys decided that. They came around us with all sorts of recommendations for their beasts, —

"Here a donkey, — he do," cried one.

"Here a good donkey, — very good," cried another.

"This is real, right donkey," shouted a third.

"Here is English Snooks donkey," ludicrously whined the next.

"Here is Yankee-Doodle donkey," enthusiastically yelled another.

This last recommendation decided me, and it was not long before I was on the back of Yankee-Doodle donkey, scampering with eight or ten of my companions, similarly mounted, through the streets of Grand Cairo.

We had not gone far, however, before a shout arrested us, and we all drew up to see what the trouble was. We found a grave, dignified man, president of a university, and his beast, were unable to agree, and both of them being somewhat mulish, in the contest had rolled over together upon the ground. When we got back to them, they had both regained their feet, and it appeared to us as if the president had lost his temper and his dignity together, while plainly enough, donkey stood laughing at him, as much as to say, — "Which is the greater jackass, — you or I?"

Again mounted, we drove to the Mosque of Mohammed Ali,

THE MAMELUKE'S LEAP.

represented by the people of Cairo to be the most gorgeous edifice on the globe. The interior, which I cannot describe, is one blaze of splendor. The effect on entering is almost overpowering. The magnificent dome, the marble pillars, the arches of polished alabaster, the rich, stained glass, the hanging lights, the tinted mosaics, lend an indescribable charm to the structure, through which we walked, according to Moslem custom, with our hats on and our shoes off, mourning at the inadequacy of language to express the admiration we felt.

The quadrangle of this mosque, overlooking the city, is memorable as the scene of one of those strokes of policy by which Mohammed Ali established himself in power, and sent terror to the hearts of his foes. Learning that a conspiracy had been formed against him by the Mamelukes, he invited six hundred of their warriors to a banquet gotten up for their destruction. They came without a suspicion of danger, but when they had assembled there, the doors of the citadel were closed upon them, and a murderous fire opened upon their doomed ranks. In vain they endeavored to break down the gates. Escape in all directions was cut off. Rank after rank fell before the fire of the concealed Albanian soldiery, until those brave warriors had all gone down before the leaden hail, and only one was left, and he, Ameen Bey, leaped his horse over a dangerous gap in the ramparts and escaped unhurt.

This was the end of that brave outlaw race, of which Napoleon Bonaparte said, — "If I could have united the Mameluke horse to the French infantry, I would have reckoned myself master of the world."

Near the mosque is Joseph's Well. It is said to have been cut in the rock by the young Hebrew ruler. For ages after, it remained filled up with rubbish, and was discovered by Sultan Joseph, quite another character, who built the citadel in 1711. These old builders certainly had an idea of greatness. Their pyramids, their monuments, and

OBELISK OF THE TEMPLE OF THE SUN, HELIOPOLIS

even their wells are vast. This one, cut in the solid rock, is two hundred and eighty feet deep, forty feet square at the top, and twenty-eight feet square at the bottom. A flight of steps cut in the stones leads from top to bottom, and the water is raised by an ox near the bottom, working the machinery which sends the water to the top. Looking down into this well seems like looking down into another world.

On our poor donkeys we scampered about that strange city, now stopping to look at a mosque, then at a street fight, then at a wrangle between a dozen women, then at some curious thing exposed for sale, then at a magician who was turning snakes into rabbits and toads into doves, having a queer time, in a hideous way.

Were my travelling companions here, they would not be satisfied, did I not refer to an incident in which I acted a prominent, but not very graceful part. While driving back, through the noisy, boisterous streets, which were wet and slippery, we all became a little excited with the novelty of our position, and driving much faster than it was safe to do with such animals, got into danger. Being in advance of my companions, one of them tried to push his donkey in front, and to save myself from contact with him, I turned in the other direction, and quite unfortunately came in contact with a donkey loaded with vegetables, a huge basket on each side. A collision took place, and quicker than I can relate it, the donkey with his load of vegetables was pitched over in one direction, while my donkey with his load of vegetables was pitched over unceremoniously in the other direction. Behind were forty half mad beasts, ridden pell-mell by forty half crazy men, and to save myself from being trampled to death, I scrambled out the best way I could, without much regard to professional dignity. I found my mutilated hat, brushed my knees with a red bandanna handkerchief, and picking up my donkey, took him home.

One day in Egypt is spent in a visit to Heliopolis, one of the most

GOING TO HELIOPOLIS.

interesting places in the land to the biblical student. It is out of Cairo, seven miles to the northeast. The city is repeatedly mentioned in Scripture, under the names of Aven, On, and Bethshemish, It is now known entirely by its Greek name. It was anciently renowned for its literature, its temples, and its priesthood. It was to Egypt what Cambridge is to England — the University city, and in its schools Plato, Solon, and Eudoxus were educated; Moses, also, was probably instructed there, in all the lore of Egypt, and fitted intellectually for that career of greatness to which God had called him. At Heliopolis, Joseph found his wife Asenath, the daughter of the Priest or Prince of On, and, from certain remains found, some have supposed that his royal residence was there.

We started out one morning in a carriage. A swift-footed forerunner went in advance, with a huge horsewhip in his hands with which he lashed dogs, donkeys, and even men and women, uttering at each turning point a peculiar warning cry, that all less important personages than ourselves might clear the way and give us free passage. Soon we all were outside of the city limits, in the oper country, and at once transported to Bible times. The same old way of drawing water; the same old way of threshing wheat; the same old way of ploughing up the ground, — no improvement in four thousand years.

The fertility of the soil is wonderful. All that is wanted is *work* and *water*. Wherever a drop of water falls, a flower, or a blade of wheat seems to spring spontaneously, and if a company of Yankee farmers, with the improvements which have been made in agricultural instruments, could take that country, they would make it in ten years the garden of the world.

At Heliopolis there is little now to see. At one time it was one of the wonders of the earth. But time has swept its glories away and little is left. One of the obelisks which formerly stood here, we have seen, was removed to Luxor, thence to Paris; two went to

Alexandria, and were dedicated to Cleopatra, but have again been removed, one to London, and the other to the Central Park in New York; three are at Rome, one adorns the terrace of St. Peter's, one

GARDEN IN HELIOPOLIS.

stands in Porta del Popolo, and the other is in the grounds of the Lateran. At Heliopolis there remains but little. The splendid temple of the sun, the groves of statues, the avenues of sphinxes, are gone, one tall obelisk, the sheik of obelisks, the Egyptians call it,

15

remains just where hands now dead placed it, four thousand years ago. The palace of the young Hebrew dreamer, the halls which Plato occupied, and which Strabo is said to have inspected as late as

MARY'S TREE.

twenty-four years B. C., are all swept away. The grand shaft bearing a monarch's name down through forty centuries alone remains.

Near Heliopolis is a tree of great age, known as Mary's tree. Under it the Virgin Mary and the infant Jesus are said to have rested in their sudden flight into Egypt. It is a tree of immense size, its boughs are all covered over with the names and initials of travellers, and may have been here in the first century, as a thrifty sycamore will live many centuries. What a comment on man! The hands which planted this tree have been paralyzed for eighteen hundred years, *but the tree still lives.* The men who sculptured yonder obelisk have been dead four thousand years, but the shaft is as perpendicular as when set up!

A day in Egypt is occupied in climbing the pyramids, and an eventful day it is. Early one morning we rode out of the city, and reached the Nile, opposite the beautiful little island of Roda, whereon tradition states that Moses was found by Pharaoh's daughter. Formerly this island was the abode of royalty, and since has been the pleasure ground to which the people have resorted for sport and recreation. The famous Nilometer on this island is an instrument to ascertain the daily rise and fall of the river. This is a matter of great importance, as the safety or destruction of the crops depend on the inundation. At certain seasons a crier in the streets of Cairo announces several times a day just how high the water is.

Dismounting we chartered a large boat with an awkward sail, and a sorry-looking crew, and naming her "Constitution," we embarked. A strange muss it was. A plank was put from the bank to the boat, and the donkeys driven in. Then the donkey boys crowded on board, for you must remember that when a man hires a donkey in Egypt he hires a boy to run behind, and *punch him!* Often a man will be riding along, not dreaming of trouble, when the boy will give the beast a vigorous prick with the goad he carries in his hand, at which the spiteful little animal will fling his heels into the air, and tumble the rider over his head as quick as a flash. The whole thing is done in an instant, the prick, the fling, and the somersault. Imagine a grave, solemn man riding along making an oration, composing poetry, thinking if he owned the pyramids what he would do with the stones, and all at once flung over the donkey's head, and landed on his back in the sand! Think of him getting up, wiping his face with his red bandanna, looking at the donkey, looking at the boy, and

A TRIP TO THE PYRAMIDS — OLD STYLE.

then mounting, looking as if he would like to kill the crowd of people who are laughing at his misfortune.

These donkey boys will run all day long beside their beasts with

FOOT OF PYRAMID.

no apparent weariness. They are the sharpest little cheats that the land contains, and from the time you take one into your service he is sponging you, in the most skilful manner, taking your pennies as a cunner will take your bait when you have a hook one-third too large, or do not know when to pull your line.

When the donkeys and boys were all in, we followed — the former taking the stern, we the bows — the boat nicely balanced. The old way of crossing was on the shoulders of human beings, who were ready to be thus used for a consideration.

Reaching the other side, and riding five or six miles over the arid plain, we come to the pyramids. These wonderful inhabitants of the desert may be described, but the impressions they produce upon the mind can never be expressed. As we approached, forty or fifty half clad Arabs came running out to meet us, and pressing their services as guides and assistants.

On arriving at the pyramids the traveller contracts with the sheik of Gizeh for persons to take him up. Four persons generally accompany each traveller. It takes four Arabs to do what one Yankee could easily perform. One takes hold of the right hand; one of the left hand; the third pushes in the rear; while the fourth carries a bottle of water to be used in case the traveller faints. The time occupied in ascending is from fifteen to thirty minutes according to the locomotive powers of the traveller. We agreed with the sheik to pay him a dollar each for the services of his men to take us to the top. Sometimes men go up without assistants, but it is dangerous unless the person is very spry, wiry, and used to climbing.

Before proceeding farther let me describe the pyramids themselves as they stand on the edge of the desert. The group we visit is three in number, though at a little distance are the pyramids of Aboo Seer, and still beyond, the pyramid of Sakhara; and farther away the pyramids of Dashoor — indeed Egypt has pyramids rising from her burning sands in all directions.

The great pyramid — Cheops, the one to which we shall now pay attention, is built upon a vast ledge of hard limestone rock, which has been excavated some ten feet or more to make the foundation. It is constructed of huge blocks of red granite, probably from the quarries of Tourah. The ledge forming a plateau is one hundred and thirty-seven feet above the level of the Nile. The pyramid was originally built in layers, forming steps, and then covered with marble or alabaster, forming a perfectly smooth surface, but the outer covering has been removed, leaving the ragged steps, which have been beaten smooth by the hand of time and the footsteps of travellers.

PYRAMID OF DASHOOR.

Cheops covers an area of thirteen acres — Boston Common has only forty-eight acres. The length of each side of the pyramid is seven hundred and fifty-seven feet: the original perpendicular height was four hundred and eighty, but the upper twenty feet have been removed. The solid contents of masonry in this immense structure amount to eighty-five million cubic feet, and the weight of the stone must be enormous.

I took up an American paper, which had reached me here on the day when I wrote this, and saw advertised several farms. One was a nice farm of ten acres; another was a pretty place of twelve acres. Another was a farm of thirteen and a half acres, just the size of the original base — a half acre having been carried away. On this place is the domicile, the barn, the flower beds, the vegetable lot, the pasturage, and all the departments of a New Jersey farm. And it is just the size of Cheops. By thinking of such a farm, how long it takes to walk over it, what is done on it, how many persons it will support, you get the best idea of the base of this pile of stone.

It is, with the top taken off, four hundred and sixty feet high. Now one of the tallest steeples in New York is that which tapers above Trinity Church on Broadway, but that is only two hundred and eighty-four feet high. Put the Grace Church spire above that, and a man swinging on the wind vane would think he was pretty well up, but let him sit on the lightning-rod there, and he would not be as high up as the original peak of Cheops. Bunker Hill monument can be seen far out to sea, and the view from its top is a wonderful panorama of cities, towns, mountains, and seas. A man on the top grows dizzy as he gazes down upon the world below. But that is only two hundred and twenty-one feet high. Lift the new Soldiers' Monument on Boston Common and let it stand on the top of Bunker Hill shaft, then add a respectable church spire to that, and you have got no higher than the pyramid.

It was mighty *Cheops* that we ascended. The number of steps is two hundred and six, formed by the layers of stone. You will see at once that the climbing must be very tedious — the steps often being but a few inches wide, and the perpendicular riser from two to six feet in height.

Everything being ready, we started up at one of the corners, winding back and forth over the angle in a zigzag direction. It is common for these villainous guides to get a traveller halfway up, and when his head reels, and he has become dizzy by looking down, to demand money of him, or threaten to leave him where he is. The day before we ascended a party of Englishmen were served this way, and all the money they had with them, about thirty pounds, extorted from them. A man halfway up, whose head begins to reel, well

ASCENT OF THE PYRAMID.

knows that he is at the mercy of the wretches. He cannot advance nor retreat without them, though with their aid a lady may ascend in perfect safety. You can conceive that a man sitting on a narrow shelf of rock, a hundred feet higher than the spire of Trinity Church, with a dizzy spell coming on, will be in a most uncomfortable position to quarrel with the guides on whom he is dependent. When he gets thoroughly frightened, as one not used to climbing, and not acquainted with Arab character and tricks, is likely to be, he is willing to give almost any sum to be taken down or carried to the top.

My Arabs started with the rest, chanting a monotonous sort of doggerel in broken English, in which was a constant demand for backsheesh. When about one-fourth of the way up, they said, " Sit

PYRAMID OF SAKHARA.

down — rest," so I sat down, and the Arabs at once demanded " Backsheesh," uttering that everlasting word sometimes in a threatening tone, and sometimes in a piteous whine. I positively refused, told them of the contract I had made with the sheik, and bade them proceed. When about half the way up, they again groaned, told me I was the heaviest man they had ever taken, and wanted *backsheesh*. But I was inexorable, and asked one of them *how much he thought I weighed?* "*Ton!* — TON!! — TON!!!" the fellow provokingly replied. On starting again, not willing to be considered the heaviest mortal that ever ascended the pyramid, I sprang as lightly as possible from step to step. Soon they wanted to rest again, and on pretence of rubbing my knees to prevent lameness, one of them got his hand on my pocket, in which was an empty purse, the condition a pedagogue's purse is generally in. At this discovery he was wild with delight. "Sovereign,"—"Napoleon," —" gold,"—"backsheesh," he shouted with the utmost enthusiasm. We were then four hundred feet from the ground, and the next effort would bring us to the top, but the guides would not proceed. They wanted one pound each as "backsheesh." At this time I had lost sight of my companions, it being a part of the Arab trick to get travellers separated, and for this purpose have different paths of ascending. Resolutely they refused to proceed, and weary and faint, I sat down on the edge of the stone, calculating my chances of ever getting to the summit. The constant demand was for *backsheesh*, which I as absolutely refused to give. I told them that if they did not wish to assist me I would go up alone. They laughed at this, and coolly told me a story, with an instructive moral to it. They said that a short time before they started up with an English gentleman, and when they had reached the very stone on which I was sitting, they demanded money, and he, indignant and angry, started on without them. On reaching the third or fourth step above where we sat, he lost his self-control, and, falling, rolled over to the bottom of the pyramid, a mangled, ghastly mass of flesh. With violent gesticulation and vehement language, they pointed to the rocks against which his lifeless body bounded as it fell, and in infernal gibberish described his awful appearance, as they found him at the base.

This recital did me good service; I had been sick for three or four days, and was in no condition to make the ascent, but the cruel, provoking manner in which they told the story, which was doubtless a lie, had the effect of the most potent tonic. Until then my courage had been oozing out of the ends of my fingers, and my head swimming with dizziness, but I was all right at once. Then ensued a little scene which I will not describe lest it savor of egotism, the result of which was that we went to the top, as fast as our feet could fly from stone to stone. I think the fellows came to the conclusion that a man pretty well frightened and desperate might use a revolver if he had one, so as to hurt somebody, even if he was not a hero.

The removal of the upper courses of stone has left a level platform about thirty feet square. Travellers, when they reach the top, do what is most natural to them. A party of ladies and gentlemen will often have a dance; some take a game of cards; some dine; some sing, and some make experiments and take observations. We took dinner there, sang "America," and "Old Hundred," carved our immortal names in the stone, and made various investigations interesting to ourselves.

It is yet a question as to the purpose for which the pyramids were erected. Some suppose they were built solely to commemorate the reign of some Egyptian sovereign. But there seems to be evidence that they were used, if not intended for scientific purposes. This was the opinion of Herschel, who gave several facts in support of the theory. I have been very much interested in the pyramidic investigations of C. Piazzi Smyth, astronomer royal for Scotland. He claims that Cheops stands apart, and is to be distinguished from all the other pyramids of Egypt, not only on account of its size, but by certain secret signs and figures which are found all over the structure, and which have been discovered wrought into stones which the builders supposed never would be exposed to view. He argues that while the work was carried on under the direction of the Egyptian government, the labor was performed by the worshippers of the true God, probably the children of Israel, for the measurements of the interior walls, and the capacity of the "great coffer," as it is called, are not according to any Egyptian standards, but compare exactly with those in use among the Jews from the earliest ages. The secret symbols carved in the stone, and the standard of measurement known first among the followers of the true God, and never recognized by the Egyptians, indicate that the Hebrew slaves, before the Exodus, were employed in their construction. It is well known that the industrial arts of Egypt, especially the sculpture and the pottery manufactures were in their hands. Vast beds of broken, crushed pottery ware are now found not far from the pyramids, though they may be of later date.

C. Piazzi Smyth says the pyramid was built in the year 2170 B. C. He obtains this number from the Pleiades, the position of which he thinks governed the location and dimensions of the passage-ways leading into the interior apartments. Herodotus dates the erection of the structure at about twenty-four hundred years B. C. The latter wrote historically, while the former follows the exactness of science. The pyramid bears the planetary configuration of the zodiac at the time of its erection, — a position the heavenly bodies have occupied but once since the creation of the world. The date of the pyramidal configuration, Piazzi Smyth finds to be 2170 B. C. The most eminent Egyptologists fix the Exodus at 1490 B. C. If these calculations are correct, the pyramids were built six hundred and eighty years before the captivity. This would exclude the idea of the work being done by the children of Israel, as their captivity lasted but four hundred and thirty years, according to Hebrew authority. But this question we leave for those who have given it attention.

Our descent was easy. The Arabs did not trouble me for backsheesh, but we went leaping down the stones at a merry rate. This was exciting, but not a little dangerous. Had the guides let go my hand for a single moment, from carelessness or anger, I should not have been here to write this letter. The sense of relief at standing again upon the solid earth was immense.

The interior of the pyramid is explored with lighted torches, at considerable risk to the neck and ribs. The structure was formerly hermetically sealed, but an entrance was effected by Caliph Mamoon in 820. The treasures he expected to find were not there, and after much work, he gave up the effort in disgust. The guides being ready with candles, we entered the narrow passage on a level with the desert sand, and by bending nearly to the floor managed to crawl down an inclined way about eighty feet. Leaving this passage, which goes down on the same angle, two hundred and twenty-five degrees, to a horizontal passage one hundred and fifty feet long, in which is an open chamber with a deep well in it, when you are more than a hundred feet below the base line of the pyramid, you ascend a passage into the grand gallery, from which proceeds at another angle, a passage leading to the Queen's Chamber, directly under the apex of the pyramid. Just at the point where the passage branches from the gallery, is the well, which descends in an irregular course to the passage which I have described below. Passing along the spacious gallery we are led to the King's Chamber, in the heart of the stony monster.

The King's Chamber is about thirty-four feet long, eighteen feet wide, and twenty feet high. Above it are several smaller rooms, designed, perhaps, as ante-rooms. The Queen's Chamber is smaller. Both are cased with red granite blocks, fitted closely and highly wrought. In the King's Chamber is the Coffer, or Sarcophagus, a stone trough, seven and a half feet long, three feet wide, and about three feet deep. It must have been placed here when the pile was in process of erection, for the passage into the chamber is too small to have allowed it to pass through. In the rooms above the King's Chamber are certain hieroglyphics painted on the stones, bearing evidence that they were brought there before the stones were placed in position. The name of Cheops is also found. And this one word, "Cheops," is his only biography; nay, the pyramid is his biography. It has stood four thousand years, and it will stand until the day of judgment, — the memorial of Cheops. But who was Cheops?

THE SPHINX.

Some one has made a calculation, that if the pyramid were excavated, and turned into a hotel, it has space enough for twenty-two thousand two hundred apartments, twelve feet square. If the structure stood in New York some of our great capitalists would doubtless utilize it in that way, or some other equally as practical.

When we came out of the pyramid we were streaming with perspiration, and covered with dust and the soft powder of the passage, which has been ground beneath pilgrim feet for a thousand years.

Near by is the Sphinx, that stupendous mystery, once an object of worship, now the wonder of every beholder. It is a huge figure, carved solid from the ledge on which it stands. The body is that of a lion, one hundred and twenty-eight feet long, in a recumbent position, now covered with desert sand. A human head and shoulders rises from the lion's breast. The circumference of the head is ninety feet. There it stands among the pyramids, looking out over the plain. We hailed it but it answered not. We inquired of it the history of deserted Gizeh, and the meaning of those mammoth piles, but it did not reply. Silent as when the Egyptians came to worship it, it stands marked and battered by the hand of time.

I must omit a description of a visit to the Petrified Forests, where are the steps of petrified palaces; another visit to the Palace of Shoobra, the old Palace of Mohammed Ali; another to the tombs of the Mameluke Kings, and to various objects of interest, and speak of life on the Nile.

I have told you in a former letter about the funeral customs of Egypt. They are very peculiar, and would shock the tastes and feelings of people in our own and European countries. But to the people here, their way of doing seems proper and best. Bodies are still embalmed, and the trade in mummy cases, which are often most elaborate and expensive, is largely carried on. We should shrink from having the dead bodies of our friends put through the process to which the bodies of the dead here are subjected, but custom makes it right.

FUNERAL PROCESSION.

The marriage customs of Egypt are, if possible, more peculiar than the funereal observances, and of all grotesque things a marriage procession is the most grotesque. "In marriage," says Dr. Randall, "the preliminary process of courtship is not called into requisition. The lady belongs to the father; he sets his price upon her, regulated according to the dignity of his own position and her beauty. She is to be bought, not won. The price is said to range from five to thirty dollars. The bargain completed, the bridegroom receives a green branch of a tree or shrub, which he sticks in his turban, and wears for three days, to show that he is espoused to a virgin. During all this time the young lady may be totally ignorant of the transaction. She comes home, perhaps, at evening, having been out, like Rebecca of old, leading her father's flocks. A short distance from the camp she

MUMMY CASES.

is met by her 'intended,' accompanied by a couple of his young friends, who adroitly seize her and carry her by force to her father's tent. In this, however, great caution and expertness are necessary, for if the damsel at all suspects their designs before they get near enough to seize her, she fights like a fury, defending herself with stones, and

MARRIAGE PROCESSION

often inflicting severe wounds, though she may not feel altogether indifferent to her lover. This defence is desert etiquette, and the more she struggles, bites, kicks and screams, the higher she ever afterwards stands in the estimation of her companions. At last vanquished and carried to her tent, one of the bridegroom's friends throws a covering over her head, and then pronounces the name of her husband, of which, up to that moment, she may have been entirely ignorant. She is then arrayed by her mother and female friends in a new costume, placed upon the back of a gaily decked camel, and though still struggling to release herself from the grasp of her husband's friends, she is paraded three times around the tent. She is then, amid the shouts of the assembled encampment, carried into the tent, and the ceremony is over."

ON THE NILE.

I started on my tour up the Nile, with the idea that I was to derive a pleasure from the excursion that could be found scarcely anywhere else, and in that was not disappointed, for every hour spent on this famous river was full of interest and pleasure. We took a boat, — a dahabieh, and began our voyage. This boat was just large enough to accommodate our party and the sailors who went with us. Two Yankee seamen would have done as well as our crew of ten, certainly one Yankee to five river Arabs. The dahabieh has a saloon, a cabin, with beds for a number of persons. The men who navigate them are not expected to want beds. They sleep on deck, or any where else that they can find a spot to lie down. The sails were very awkward ones, but sufficient for the purpose.

Our first landing was at Bedresbayn, whence we proceeded to the ruins of ancient Memphis. Perhaps the object of the greatest interest in this detour made from the boat is the Stepped Pyramid, which is thought by some to be older than Gizeh. When Joseph was in Egypt, Memphis, now in ruins, was the capital, and the residence of the king. Cairo is comparatively of modern origin, but

IN EGYPT.   245

Memphis dates back to those days when pyramids were built, and the Pharaohs were on the Egyptian throne, and that land, now so fallen, was the patron of art and literature, and men came from all parts of the world to behold its glory.

Still floating on we have a fine opportunity to become acquainted with the climate, people, and natural scenery of the country. Along

NILE BOAT.

the Nile are the various modes of drawing water from the river, for the purpose of irrigation. The familiar water-wheel meets the eye very frequently, and the shadoof is seen working in its primitive way, doubtless as it did in the times of Joseph.

We become acquainted with the birds, fishes, and sometimes too familiarly with the reptiles of the river. We float along close to the shore, where several crocodiles are seen lying lazily in the hot sun, and some of them are so huge that it seems as if their open jaws might crush the little boat, and annihilate it with its occupants. But the ugly creatures do not trouble you unless you trouble them. It would hardly be safe, however, to be found amongst them on the shore. They are savage fellows, and do not allow any familiarities.

While the monsters form an unpleasant feature of Nile scenery, the beautiful flowers growing on the banks, or floating on the surface,

STEPPED PYRAMID.

are very attractive. The lotos growing in the water was once one of the most common of Egyptian plants. The flower was used for decorations on all occasions. At funerals, at weddings, at religious festivals it was seen. On the tombs and monuments of the dead, it is often found engraved. But it has disappeared. In some dry season, it withered and died out. The papyrus, which was also so very common ages ago, is gone.

It is very easy to see how the plants should disappear from some parts of Egypt, but why water plants should die out of the Nile, and the seed be lost, is not quite so plain.

At Thebes and Karnac, we saw the glories of ancient ruins. It is hard for imagination to depict the beauties of these ancient palaces and halls when they were in their early elegance.

WATER-WHEEL.

"Thebes," says one writer, "must have been the greatest and most magnificent city in Egypt. Almost as old as the flood, situated in a fertile valley, where it expanded to a vast and splendid amphitheatre, and adorning both banks of the Nile, it was in extent, wealth, and architectural glory, the flower and crown of ancient civilization. Nearly a thousand years before Christ, Homer sang of its hundred gates, and some of the Sacred Prophets speak of it as being 'populous,' or containing a 'multitude.' No one can visit its present unparalleled ruins, or linger among the gorgeous mausoleums of its kings and princes, without being deeply impressed with a sense of its former vastness and grandeur. The contrast suggested by the present Thebes, a miserable representative even of Arab filth and squalidness, is overwhelmingly powerful; and the imagination is

NILE MONSTERS.

continually struggling to restore and repeople the city, and look upon its splendor ere it was devastated by the Persian conqueror. But these mournful relics and the utter desolation of the once imperial metropolis teach most impressive lessons.

> 'Thousands of years have rolled along,
>   And blasted empires in their pride;
> And witnessed scenes of crime and wrong,
>   Till men by nations died.
>
> Thousands of summer-suns have shone,
>   Till earth grew bright beneath their sway,
> Since thou, untenanted and lone,
>   Wert rendered to decay.'"

The wish comes instinctively that we could see these cities rise again, and in their early magnificence stand before us. But that is never to be. Rome may rise from its ruins; Jerusalem may become the metropolis of wealth and power again, but Karnac and Thebes can never rise. They are too far from the paths

LOTOS.

of commerce, too remote from the centres of trade, too near the burning sands of the desert, to suit the progress of modern life.

Concerning the grand temple at Karnac, the writer from whom I have just quoted, and whose work I had in my hand as I walked amid those stupendous ruins, says: "A mile and a half north of Luxor are the ruins of Karnac, the grandest temple in Egypt, if not in the world. I visited it just about evening, enjoying as I returned as gorgeous a sunset as mortal vision could desire. Ah! what varied scenes, what splendid pageants, what ages of glory and decay, that setting sun has witnessed here. It is impossible

PAPYRUS.

PROPYLON AT KARNAC.

to describe Karnac. One must see it, or he will have no adequate idea of its astonishing magnitude and beauty. Such an array of massive gates, towers, columns, obelisks, and statues is a perfect marvel. Think of a temple, including its various halls and apartments, twelve hundred feet long, and about five hundred feet wide, its massive walls rising

COLUMN OF THOTHMES III.

like palisades, and its immense pillars like forests, with avenues leading to it from each point of the compass, along which, in some instances for miles, were ranged double rows of colossal sphinxes of gray, red, and black granite. The edifice is said to have occupied about seventy-five acres, it having been enlarged from time to time, by different monarchs, each striving to outdo his predecessor. In the grand hall there are still standing over a hundred columns, nine to twelve feet in diameter, and many of them over sixty feet high. All are covered with various hieroglyphical sculptures and paintings, whose colors are still bright after the lapse of nearly forty centuries. In one place you see a group of Jews led captive by an Egyptian king. The characters interpreted agree with the Bible account of Shishak's victory over the King of Judah, — a striking verification of the sacred record."

In floating along the Nile, the traveller accustomed to the matter-of-fact scenes of American or European travel, seems to be in a constant dream, from which he is seldom aroused. The customs of the people, and the antiquity of the different objects, give an idea of unreality to everything

Not a few of the customs would furnish the boys of the Triangle room for mirth. But of them I must tell you at some other time. We kept the Nile until near its head waters beyond the cataracts, and then our party returned, leaving me to pursue my journey alone through Nubia, Abyssinia, and Zanzibar.

RIP VAN WINKLE.

IN SOUTHERN AFRICA.

GYPSY TENT.

"Good-bye, gentlemen," said Rip Van Winkle, as his late friends and fellow travellers stood on board their boat to go down the Nile, leaving him at Aboo Sambool or Ipsamboul.

The "good-bye" was returned.

"May you have as pleasant a voyage down the Nile as we have had up."

"And may you have a fine tour through the country to your destination."

"Farewell."

"Farewell," came back from the boat in a chorus of voices.

The little craft was soon gliding down the stream, and the Master saw his friends no more. With a somewhat sad face he turned away to make arrangements for a long and tedious journey to the distant coast. We will let him speak for himself.

ZANZIBAR.

A long leap from the Nile! And a hard leap you would have said if you had taken it. At Aboo Sambool, the first party with

TEMPLE OF IPSAMBOUL.

which I had been travelling, concluded to turn back to Cairo; I concluded to keep on.

Ipsamboul is on the west side of the Nile, in Nubia, and has some very perfect specimens of ancient temples. The great temple, so-called, is a marvellous ruin, the carved figures being distinguished yet for their expressiveness and beauty. Some one says of them, "The masterpieces of Greece, higher in rank, have nothing to match with the mystic beauty of these."

Before leaving the Nile entirely, I know the boys will wish me to say something about that which will interest them more than ruin and effigies however magnificent. I can imagine a flood of questions.

"Did you have any hunting or shooting on the Nile," I think I hear Hal ask.

"O yes, plenty of it. The birds of Egypt are very numerous i-

ONE OF THEM.

variety, and are easily shot. Some of the birds are sacred, and their destruction is prohibited. But others can be taken without restriction."

"What kind of birds are they?" perhaps Hal asks.

Storks, cranes, pelicans, ducks, herons, pigeons, geese, and smaller birds are plenty enough for any sportsman. An Englishman who visited Egypt for sporting and remained there two months, is reported to have shot five thousand five hundred and seventy-six birds in all, of which one thousand five hundred and fourteen were wild geese. Partridge and quails are found all along the river.

"What kind of fish did you find?" perhaps Will asks.

ELECTRIC SHAD.

Well, we were fortunate in fish, also. The Nile has many varieties, and they are taken with hook, net, and spear.

"What are they?" do you ask.

Well, there is the electric shad, a nice fellow that will give you

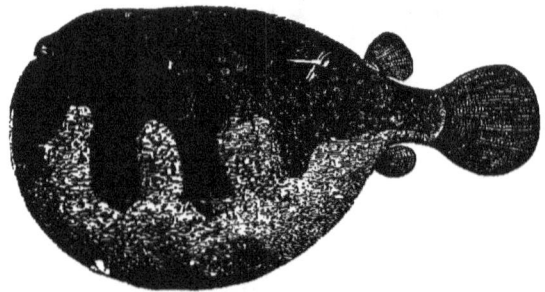

TETRODON.

a shock that will make your arm ache if you touch him. Then there is the tetrodon, which some one says "looks like a pumpkin with a tail," twinkling eyes, and a little laughing mouth with four teeth. He is the most funny fish I ever saw Then there are the kanooma, and the finny pike, which are taken in large quantities, and are sold in the fish markets by dealers, who do a large business."

But enough for fish and fowl. After the party had left me, I went to the place where an English official had an office for the transaction of business, and made inquiries as to how I should reach this

KANOOMA.

place, and after much conversation, concluded to take a couple of Nubian dragomen, and go through without waiting for the chance of friendly company of my own color. I was directed to a Bedouin and his son, who were trusty, and who were well acquainted with the country. I found them sitting in their tent, and told them what I

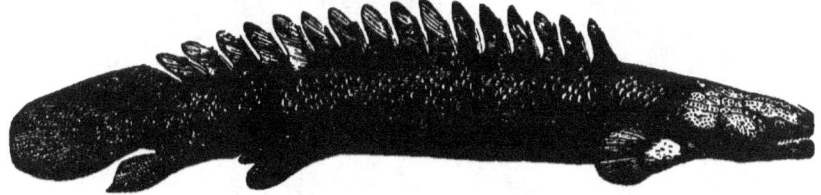

INNY PIKE.

wanted. They were ready to go, and on the third day after, three camels and their riders started across the country. The two dragomen whom I had hired were very pleasant and agreeable men, and knew enough of English to make themselves understood in that language. Aboo, the father, seemed scarcely older than his son, and yet the son was a model of respectful reverence for his sire worthy the imitation of the boys in our country. The name of the son was Selim. He was quick, active, and had a fine eye. Would you like to see Aboo and Selim? Here they are.

ABOO AND SELIM.

The journey was a long one, at times by land, and at times by water, exchanging our camels for boats; a part of the way inland, and a part of the way along the coast. Aboo and Selim were faithful to the end, and after paying them for their services I parted from them with regret.

On reaching Zanzibar,—which is the chief town of an island of the same name, on the southeast coast of Africa, separated by a narrow creek of water from Zanguebar, the main land,—I repaired to an inn which is the resort of British and American seamen, where I found a rough but honest crowd of people, representing these two nations. The place is said to have thirty thousand inhabitants, made up of several distinct nationalities. The town is distinguished for its trade in slaves, and in other days when the traffic in human beings was more brisk than it now is, a great number of blacks were brought here to be shipped to other nations.

LIFE IN THE INTERIOR.

The exports consist of ivory, hides, tortoise shell, dates, pepper, gum, sugar, coffee, and other articles. It is common to see the flags of a half dozen nations waving in the harbor.

The houses are poor, being built of very light materials, those in which the negro population live being of bamboo, covered with palm-leaves. There are few buildings of even moderate pretensions to elegance outwardly, judged from a European standpoint.

ZANZIBAR.

It was not my purpose to stay here long, and quickly as possible I arranged to leave. I found a vessel under an American flag, bound to Madagascar, and was soon on the way. Zanzibar, as seen from the sea, is very pretty; and yet, gazing over from the stern of the vessel, I could not regret that I was leaving it far behind me, never to see it again.

MADAGASCAR.

Our vessel, after a few terrific squalls, brought us to Tamatave, which is, perhaps, the most important seaport on the east coast. I proceeded at once to see what was possible of the island, which is the largest of the African islands, having an area of two hundred and forty thousand square miles of territory, a great part of which is dense forest. Walking along a street in Tamatave does not remind one of the fashionable streets of our own cities. I found the people very hospitable and kind, much more so than at Zanzibar, and every facility was furnished me to see all I could of the island. And this was not much, for while there was not much to see in the towns, I was not prepared to venture much into the interior. The natives of the interior are hardly to be trusted by a single-handed and unprotected stranger.

The rivers swarm with crocodiles, compared to which, in length and ferocity, those of the Nile are said to be insignificant. The forests are filled with wild animals, and large birds, while the lesser inhabitants, monkeys, foxes, squirrels, dogs, cats, wild hogs, baboons and wolves, are very common. Outside the town, the traveller, by day and by night is obliged to encounter huge serpents, some of which are quite venomous and dangerous. So you can see that the interior of Madagascar would not be a very beautiful place for a summer residence or a country home. The fruits are very fine. Bread-fruit, bananas, plantains, yams, oranges, peaches, and other kinds of fruit abound. The cocoa-nut here grows to great size and excellence. The foliage is rich, and where it does not hide some biting, stinging creature, it furnishes delight, fragrance and shelter to man. The native homes, found scattered all over this island, are not models of architecture, but they are comfortable to live in and not unpleasant to the eye. The climate allows of the most meagre shelter at night, and the natives do not care to have anything more inserted in their homes than is absolutely required. As the interior is reached, the houses are found to be mere huts in which the creatures may crouch and be protected from the scorching sun of noonday, and from the wild beasts that are liable to make an unceremonious visit at night.

The natives are low in the scale of being. "Their mental faculties," says a writer who has thoroughly examined their condition, "though, in a majority of cases, deteriorated by sensuality, enfeebled and cramped in their exercise by the juggleries of divination and sorcery, and the absurdities of superstition, are yet such as to warrant the conclusion that they are not inferior to other portions of the human race; that if liberated from the debasing trammels by which they are now confined, and favored with enlightened and generous culture, they are capable of high mental excellence. Among the dark colored races, the Sakalavas manifest the greatest intellectual vigor, uniting a remarkable quickness of perception with soundness of judgment." As much as this might be said of the freedmen of the Southern States of America. But it would not mark the average freedman with high intellectual qualities, whatever might be the result of years of improvement.

STREET IN TAMATAVE.

We have seen it stated that the people of Madagascar are terribly given to lying, that truth seems to be the exception rather than the rule, that lying is not regarded as a vice or a defect of character, but if done adroitly, an excellence, and that when the Gospel was preached among them at first, it was opposed on the ground that it taught people to tell the truth, and condemned falsehood. I incline to the opinion that deception is characteristic of all the African races that I have seen. Those tribes that are kind and hospitable to strangers, a..d that live at peace among themselves, are given to lying and deception to a fearful extent. But while given to lying, they are, to a great extent, free from the evils of strong drink. Drunkenness is seldom seen in any of the interior villages. Where white men have set up trade, there liquor is found and drank, but where the Madagascans have control, temperance is the rule. It is very unusual

FOLIAGE IN MADAGASCAR.

to see a native drunk. This should be said to their commendation. The seaports, however, show the same amount of drunkenness that is witnessed wherever European or American seamen are found in large numbers. As at Tangier, Algiers, Tripoli and Alexandria, so it is at Tamatave.

The capital of Madagascar is Tananarivo, a considerable place of nearly thirty thousand inhabitants, and with more of the characteristics of a city than most of the towns, even on the coast.

Two or three excursions into the interior gave me some view of the inside life of the people. The rice is cultivated very extensively, and forms a principal article of food among all classes, and you are often asked to eat it with the kindly native, who means by eating with you to express hospitality. To eat with a Madagascan means friendship. To refuse is to menace, and reject friendship. So when

CHIEF'S HOUSE, TAMATAVE.

invited to eat, I, of course complied, and once or twice the only helps in the process were the fingers, the Madagascan on one side of the bowl and the American on the other. It is much easier to eat bananas or oranges with the natives than to eat rice. With these articles the fingers are much more useful than in the disposition of rice.

There are many things eaten by the natives that we should reject. While their fowls and fruit are delicious, the dried locusts and the roasted lizards are rather repugnant to our ideas of things. The former are boiled, and eaten with great relish.

Though Madagascar is far more peaceful and better mannered

MADAGASCANS.

than it was a few years ago, the island is far from being civilized. The Gospel religion has done much to change the ferocity of the people into habits of peace, and the practices which prevailed a half century ago have given place to a general recognition of Christianity, as a religion at least to be tolerated.

I filled up two or three weeks in visits to the principal cities mainly on the eastern coast, in two or three excursions into the interior, and in the general study of the island, in its climate, productions and people, and prepared to leave.

But no one can be in Madagascar any length of time without an appreciation of what has been done for the island by the Christian religion. An instance of this is given by Rev. J. Sibree, who lived among this people nearly a score of years. "Some six years ago," he says, " the central government felt it to be necessary to send an army to put down an insurrection; but, before the army went away, the prime minister called the officers together, and said, 'Now, you are going to fight with the queen's enemies, but remember they are the queen's people, too. You know how we carried on war in former times; but remember, you are Christians now, and the cruelties of heathen times are not to be done again.' Well, that army went away, and one division of it was able to pacify the country without taking a single life. The native chief was invited to the tent of the commander, and here he was shown a New Testament; the commander said, ' This is the Book from which we Christians learn what is right, and, according to this Book, we never put to death or punish the upright, as we often did when we were heathen; but the guilty must be punished, for this is the word of God and the law of the queen.' The following day there was another interview, terms of peace were agreed upon,
beautiful copy of the New Testament was given to the native chief,
.l the commander said to him, 'If ever we make war upon you without just cause, or kill or punish the guiltless, show us this Book, then, indeed we shall be self-condemned.'"

One would hardly realize such a change on a heathen island, where a little while ago the blood of the helpless martyrs was flowing in torrents, — an island toward which the whole world looked with emotions of horror. But the change is a fact in which every lover of his race may well rejoice. And the same agency is lifting other communities, and giving them position and power among the nations of the earth. Paganism has done nothing for the world but to debase

INTERIOR OF MADAGASCAR.

it. As that disappears before the civilization of a Christian age, the world grows better and purer. Of these things you will know more as you grow older, and see more of the changes which are taking place among the nations. "The better day coming" is not merely a dream. It is not an idea that exists entirely in the visions of poets, but it is a substantial fact that meets us from pole to pole. "The better day coming!" Well, the world will be ready to hail it when it arrives.

Rip Van Winkle.

IN INDIA.

BUDDHIST TEMPLE, LAKE OF KANDY.

"WHERE are you bound?" asked Rip Van Winkle of the captain of a fine brig that was almost ready to sail from the harbor of Tamatave.

"For Ceylon."

"Do you take passengers?"

"We only take passengers as a matter of accommodation to them."

"Have you any for this voyage?"

"Two, a gentleman and his wife."

"Do you wish to take another?"

"Do you wish to go?"

"Yes, will you take me?"

"If you will put up with such accommodations as we can offer; our brig is not fitted up in sumptuous style, though her accommodations will not be very bad."

"I will take the risk and go with you."

"We shall sail to-morrow."

"I can be ready. A man who does not carry much baggage, but who contents himself with a small carpet bag, can soon be off from any place."

"We will do the best we can for you. But your name, sir?"

"My name?"

The master had to stop a moment to think what it was. It was so long since he had heard it spoken that he was obliged to pause before giving it.

"Rip Van Winkle."

"What a name! — any relation to the original Rip?"

"No, none whatever."

"Well, Rip Van Winkle will find himself booked for a passage when he gets on board to-morrow morning."

The voyage proved to be a very pleasant one. The lady and gentleman passengers were a missionary and his wife, the latter in poor health, but the weather being pleasant, the trio, — Rip Van Winkle having speedily become acquainted with the other two, — were able to be on deck almost every day, and in reading and pleasant conversation the time slipped off, and each one was sorry when the outlines of Ceylon were seen in the distance. Following is the letter which the master wrote to his young friends from India.

CEYLON.

It will be impossible for me to describe the pleasurable emotions I experienced when I found myself among some college chums who had reached Ceylon by quite another route, and who were destined to be my associates in travelling through the country. Our brig brought us to Colombo, where I parted with the passengers and crew, with less regret than if I had not at once found my American friends, with whom I commenced explorations.

If you look on your maps you will see where Ceylon is, and be able to follow me as I skip about from place to place. "Ceylon in shape and position," says Mr. Urwick, "hangs like a pear from the southeast coast of the Indian Peninsula. The isthmus called Adam's Bridge forms as it were the stalk connecting the island with the continent; the name Adam's Bridge arising from the Mohammedan legend that on his expulsion from Paradise, Adam passed by this singular causeway into Ceylon. The isthmus connects Ramisseram with Manaar, and is cut in one place only by a channel called the Paumban Passage, through which vessels drawing ten feet may pass, but larger ships and steamers to and from Madras and Bombay must go all the way round Ceylon. The northern portion, answering to the thin part of the pear, is one vast forest — interminable jungle — dotted sparsely with specks of yellow-green cultivation, but containing the ruins of two ancient capitals, and on the east coast, the port of Trincomalee. The lower half of the island swells out in the Kandyan provinces into a mass of gneiss and granite mountains, with a margin of rich and luxuriant lower land; and here we find the best scenery, and the chief centres of modern enterprise. Almost in the middle of the island is the capital Kandy, connected by railway with Colombo on the west coast; and on the southwest corner is the well-known port of call, Point de Galle.

"To the sea-trained eye of the voyager across the hot Indian Ocean from the east or west, Ceylon unfolds a scene of loveliness and grandeur unsurpassed by any land. It enjoys two monsoons in the year, and the abundant supply of moisture thus afforded, clothes it with perpetual green. Its slopes are enamelled with verdure; flowers of gorgeous hues deck its plains, palms of all descriptions abound, climbing plants rooted in the rocks hang down in huge festoons, and trees dip their foliage into the sea. By the Brahmins the island was called Lanka, 'the resplendent;' by the Buddhists 'a pearl upon the brow of India;' by the Chinese 'the island of jewels;' by the Greeks 'the land of the hyacinth and the ruby.' It has with reason been regarded as the country whither the ships of Solomon came for 'gold and silver, ivory, and apes, and peacocks.'"

Colombo is a large city, and has one hundred and fifty thousand inhabitants. Its early name was Kalambee, but was altered to Colombo in honor of the discoverer of America. For this we may thank the Portuguese. And other changes have been made by Portuguese, Dutch and English for which we may be thankful. The three nations have, in time, had possession, the latter power ruling here since 1796.

Among the products of the region is the cocoanut, and the tall trees are found everywhere. It would be just the spot, though somewhat hazardous, for a Yankee boy to climb these trees and gather the fruit. "Like the Palmyra tree in the north of Ceylon," says the author just quoted, — "the cocoa-nut in the south yields most of the necessaries of life. Its fruit furnishes food, its shell drinking vessels, its juice palm wine and sugar, its stem materials for building, its leaves roofs, matting, baskets and paper. The number of these trees in the island is estimated to be twenty millions. The natives climb them with great agility, partly with the help of bamboo ladders, and oftener with the help of a short band of cocoa-nut fibre between the feet or round the loins. In Colombo the raw coffee brought from the plantations undergoes the process of curing at several mills for the purpose. Here may be seen first, the drying of the beans; secondly, the removal of the skin by passing the beans under rollers; thirdly, the picking out of the bad berries, done by women and children; fourthly, the distribution of the different sizes by means of sieves; fifthly, the process of packing in barrels for transportation." The town is fortified, and defended against any not very considerable force.

A FOREST OF ELEPHANTS

The temperature is very moderate and even, averaging in summer 80° and in winter about 70°. The commercial advantages of the place make it the most important of the seaport towns.

Kandy (or Candi) is about seventy-five miles inland. It is the capital of the central province, and is the Mecca of Ceylon. It has

KANDY.

ten thousand inhabitants located on several hills. The city is very beautiful, and one thousand six hundred and seventy-eight feet above the level of the sea. The Buddhists have a tradition that when Adam left Paradise he rested with one foot on one of the mountains on which Kandy is located, now called Adam's peak. On one of the boulders on the summit is the impression of a vast human foot.

Adam must have been a giant if this legend is true, for the footprint is five feet and one half long and two feet and one half broad. There are not a few sacred objects, which are held in great reverence by the Mohammedans and Buddhists. The sacred tooth of Buddha is guarded with great care. At Anurajapura is the sacred Bo-tree, said to be twenty-one hundred years old, which draws pilgrims from distant lands to see it, and sit in its shadow.

The ancient temples are characteristic of Buddhism, and emblematic of its decay. At Matale, Anurajapura, Pulastipura, and other places these structures are found. Christianity is making them useless.

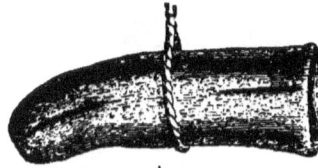

BUDDHA'S TOOTH.

The Gar-urhava at Pulastipura is "a rock temple, which has in front four richly-carved columns, a raised altar, with a statue of Buddha seated, a statue of Buddha standing, and a statue of the same famous saint reclining — forty-five feet in length — the attitude of his attaining Nirvana."

The boys, were they here with me, would find many things that are seldom seen in America, — never unless they have been imported. Elephants and india-rubber trees abound. Crocodiles and scorpions are quite common. Elephant hunts are frequent, and sportsmen from other parts of the world come here to take part in them. All kinds of tropical fruits and flowers are found in great abundance everywhere Everywhere we are reminded of Heber's hymn, —

> "What though the spicy breezes
> Blow soft o'er Ceylon's isle,
> Though every prospect pleases,
> *And only man is vile.*"

MADRAS.

From Ceylon to Madras, — on every side are evidences of the prevalent religion of India, Buddhism. Dr. Malcom says, — "Buddhism is, probably, at this time and has been for many centuries, the most prevalent form of religion upon earth. Half of the population of China, Lao, Cochin-China, and Ceylon; all of Camboja, Siam, Burmah, Thibet, Tartary, and Loo-choo; and a great part of Japan,

TEMPLE OF THE DALADA.

and most of the other islands of the southern seas, are of this faith. A system which thus enchains the minds of half the human race deserves the attention of both Christians and philosophers, however fabulous and absurd. Chinese accounts make the introduction of Buddhism into that empire to have occurred about A. D. 65. Marshman supposes the Siamese and Laos to have received the system about three centuries before Christ. A very great increase of the Buddhist faith is known to have occurred in China early in the sixth century, which may have resulted from the flight of priests with him, about that time, from the persecution of the Brahminists.

MADRAS SURF.

Buddh is a general term for divinity, and not the name of any particular god. There have been innumerable Buddhs, in different ages, among different worlds, but in no world more than five, and in some, not any. In this world, there have been four Buddhs, viz., Kan-ka-than, Gau-na-gang, Ka-tha-pa, and Gaudama. In the Siamese language, these are called Kak-a-san, Ko-na-gon, Kasap, and Kodom. One is yet to come, viz., Aree-ma-day-eh. It has been often remarked, that Gaudama was one of the incarnations of Vishnu, and appeared in the form of a cow. This idea has probably originated with the Hindus, and is advanced to support their assertion, that this religion is a branch of theirs. "But no two systems can be more opposite, or bear less evidence of one being derived from the other. Brahminism has incarnations, but Buddhism admits of none, for it has no permanent God. If, in its endless metempsychosis, any being should descend from the highest forms of existence, to take human nature, it would not be an incarnation of Deity, but a real degradation of being, and the person so descending would become, *literally*, a man. If he ever rise again, it must be by another almost infinite change, now to better, and now to worse, as a merit is gained or lost. While Hinduism teaches one eternal deity, Buddhism has now no god. That has a host of idols; this only one. That enjoins bloody sacrifices; this forbids all killing."

The same authority gives us an idea of the last Buddh: — "Gaudama was the son of Thoke-daw-da-reh, or, as it is written in Sanscrit, Soodawdaneh, king of Ma-ge-deh, (now called Behar,) in Hindustan. He was born about B. C. 626. He had previously lived in four hundred millions of worlds, and passed through innumerable conditions in each. In *this* world he had been almost every sort of worm, fly, fowl, fish, or animal, and almost every grade and condition of human life. Having, in the course of these transitions, attained immense merit, he at length was born son of the above-named king. The moment he was born, he jumped upon his feet, and, spreading out his arms, exclaimed, 'Now am I the noblest of men! This is the last time I shall ever be born!' His height, when grown up, was nine cubits. His ears were so beautifully long, as to hang upon his shoulders; his hands reached to his knees; his fingers were of equal length; and with his tongue he could touch the end of his nose! All which, are considered irrefragable proofs of his divinity. When in this state, his mind was enlarged, so that he remembered his former conditions and existences. Of these he rehearsed many to his followers. Five hundred and fifty of these narratives have been preserved, one relating his life and adventures as a deer, another as a monkey, elephant, fowl, etc. The collection is called *Dzat*, and forms a very considerable part of the sacred books. These legends are a fruitful source of designs for Burman paintings. Of these I purchased several, which do but bring out into visible absurdity the system they would illustrate. He became Buddh in the thirty-fifth year of his age, and remained so forty-five years, at the end of which time, having

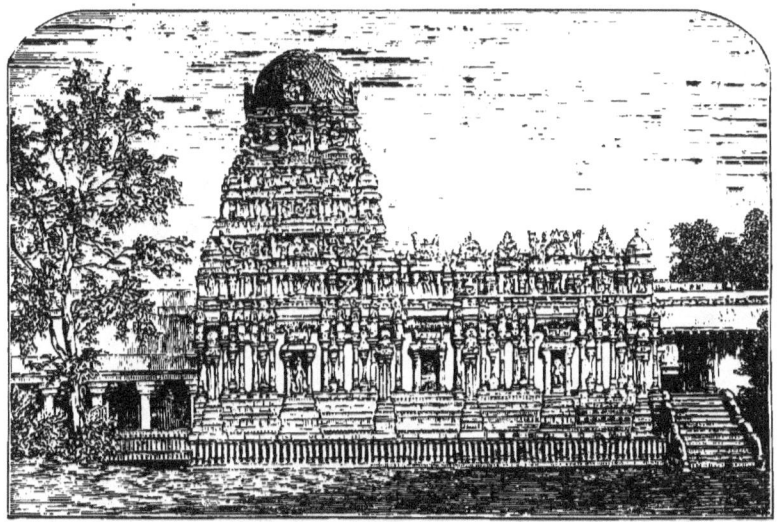

TEMPLE OF SOUBRAMANYA, TANJORE.

performed all sorts of meritorious deeds, and promulgated excellent laws, far and wide, he obtained 'nicban,' that is, entered into annihilation, together with five hundred priests, by whom he had been long attended. This occurred in Hindustan, about two thousand three hundred and eighty years ago, or B. C. 546."

With the religion of India, Christianity is now competing. The Baptists who were early in the field, and the English and American Boards have wrought great changes. We are told that at "Madura, the American Board has a very efficient mission, with valuable schools. It was founded in 1834; since which time it has covered the entire province with a network of stations. It includes one hundred and thirty-eight congregations, a hundred native missionaries,

ROCK TEMPLE, TRICHINOPOLY.

and a hundred native teachers. The institution of boarding-schools, peculiar to missions in Southern India, was introduced by the American Board, and there are in the Madura province one hundred and eighteen schools and training colleges."

The tramp of British civilization is seen in railroads, beaten turnpikes, and other signs of improvement. Such beautiful towns as Madura, Trichinopoly, and Tanjore, are all about us.

Madras is the capital of the presidency of the same name, and is well located on the shores of the Bay of Bengal. It has nearly a million inhabitants, and extends along the shores of the bay about ten miles, and is a somewhat beautiful city. The public buildings owned by the British government are generally fine structures. The pagodas and temples are conspicuous. But the private residences are not of any particular attractiveness. The city has no harbor. As at many Mediterranean ports, vessels must anchor out in the bay, and lighters are used to load and unload. The fortifications are complete. Fort St. George is one of the strongest defences in India. A thousand men can be accommodated within its walls. The gas-lighted streets are kept in good condition, and the traveller has abundant reason to be thankful for British rule. Of course many sights are seen, and sounds heard in the streets which are novel to an American. The flower-sellers, the milk merchants, the vendors of various kinds of produce, all have their peculiar cries, and are heard at all times from one end of the city to the other.

TANJORE.

Tanjore is one hundred and eighty miles southwest of Madras, a city of eighty thousand inhabitants. It lies back a considerable distance from the coast. As a seat of British power it is well fortified, but retains more of the distinctive characteristics of modern life and character than do the seaport towns. It is famous for an immense granite bull which stands over the main entrance to the city, a very notable piece of workmanship, which some day will come crashing down. The streets are narrow, the inhabitants ignorant, and governed by a caste that holds its supremacy against all the light of the present age. The traveller will get into Tanjore and get out as soon as he can. The temple dedicated to Hindoo worship is one of the attractions. The fort is another. The palace adds more interest, but on the whole Tanjore cannot be said to be an attractive place. At Tranquebar, in the province of Tanjore, the Catholics and the Lutherans have made some progress against the religion of the country, and each of these sects have schools and churches with a

SELLERS OF MILK, MADRAS.

large following. Like Tanjore, Tranquebar is on the river Cavery. Pondicherry, between Tanjore and Madras, shows its French affiliations. There are no fortifications, the building of them having been disallowed by the English, when in 1803 they gave up the city to its French owners. The landing of soldiers is also prohibited. Before war devastated it, it is said to have been one of the most elegant of all the Indian cities.

PAGODA AT PONDICHERRY.

CALCUTTA.

In a coasting vessel we reached Calcutta from Madras, sailing up the Hoogly, to find an improvement in all that constitutes physical comfort. "There being no wharves or docks," says Malcom, "you are rowed to a ghaut in a dingey, and landed amid Hindoos performing their ablutions and reciting their prayers. No sooner does your boat touch the shore, than a host of bearers contend for you with loud jabber, and those whom you resist least, actually bear you off on their arms through the mud, and you find yourself at once in one of those strange conveyances, a palankeen. Away you hie, flat on your back, at the rate of nearly five miles an hour, a chatty boy bearing aloft a huge palm-leaf umbrella to keep off the sun, whom no assurances that you do not want him will drive away, but who expects only a pice or two for his pains. The bearers grunt at every step, like southern negroes when cleaving wood; and though they do it as a sort of chorus, it keeps your unaccustomed feelings discomposed.

"Arrived at the house, you find it secluded within a high brick wall, and guarded at the gate by a durwan, or porter, who lives there in a lodge, less to prevent ingress, than to see that servants and others carry nothing away improperly. The door is sheltered by a porch, called here a veranda, so constructed as to shelter carriages — a precaution equally necessary for the rains and the sun. The best houses are of two stories, the upper being occupied by the family, and the lower used for dining and store rooms. On every side are contrivances to mitigate heat and exclude dust. Venetian blinds enclose the veranda, extending from pillar to pillar, as low as a man's head. The remaining space is furnished with mats, (tatties,) which reach to the floor, when the sun is on that side, but at other times are rolled up. When these are kept wet, they diffuse a most agreeable coolness. The moment you sit down, whether in a mansion, office, or shop, a servant commences pulling the punka, under which you may happen to be. The floor is of brick and mortar, covered with mats, the walls of the purest white, and the ceilings of great height. Both sexes, and all orders, dress in white cottons. The rooms are kept dark, and in the hottest part of the day shut up with glass. In short, everything betrays a struggle to keep cool."

TRAVELLING IN INDIA.

The methods of travelling, in spite of railroads and modern means of locomotion are quite as curious as is the donkey riding of Egypt. Cows and bullocks are harnessed into queer-looking vehicles, and fat, portly men ride along through the country and over the roads as if they had the whole generation to work in. Nobody hurries who ought to, and everybody hurries that ought not to. "A walk in the native town," says the author just quoted, " presents novel sights on every side. The houses, for the most part, are mere hovels, with mud floors and mud walls, scarcely high enough to stand up in, and covered with thatch. The streets are narrow, crooked, and dirty;

and on every neglected wall, cow dung, mixed with chaff, and kneaded into thin cakes, is stuck up to dry for fuel. The shops are often but six or eight feet square, and seldom twice this size, wholly open in front, without any counter, but the mat on the floor, part of which is occupied by the vendor, sitting cross-legged, and the

BULLOCK CARRIAGE.

rest serves to exhibit his goods. Mechanics have a similar arrangement.

"Barbers sit in the open street on a mat, and the patient, squatting on his hams, has not only his beard, but part of his head, shaved, leaving the hair to grow only on his crown. In the tanks and ponds are dobies slapping their clothes with all their might upon a bench or a stone. Little braminy bulls, with their humped shoulders, walk among the crowd, thrusting their noses into the baskets of rice, grain,

A RELIGIOUS BEGGAR

or peas, with little resistance, except they stay to repeat the mouthful. Bullocks, loaded with panniers, pass slowly by. Palankeens come bustling along, the bearers shouting at the people to clear the way. Peddlers and hucksters utter their ceaseless cries. Religious mendicants, with long hair matted with cow dung, and with faces and arms smeared with Ganges mud, walk about almost naked, with an air of the utmost impudence and pride, demanding rather than begging gifts. Often they carry a thick triangular plate of brass, and, striking it at intervals with a heavy stick, send the shrill announcement of their approach far and near. Now and then comes rushing along the buggy of some English merchant, whose syce, running before, drives the pedestrians out of the way; or some villanous-looking caranche drags by, shut up close with red cloth, containing native ladies, who contrive thus to 'take the air.'" This description, though written some time since, is accurate to-day.

A novel Calcutta character is the religious mendicant, who meets you when you least expect him, and sues for your generous contribution to his wants. He is often a striking figure, combining the gravity of the judge, the serenity of the priest, the learned look of the philosopher and the cunning of the mountebank. When you meet him in the streets you hardly know what to make of him, or with what division of the people to class him.

The Thugs are not so often found in India as they formerly were, though now and then they are met. Their very name is a terror, and their instruments of torture and death have made them a class so hated even by the milder natives that eventual extermination must be their fate. Mr. Urwick says the "Thugs, who abounded chiefly in the forests, were fanatics who made highway robbery part of their religion, and declared that their victims were sacrifices to the goddess Kali. Disguised as peaceful travellers, they would first engage in simple and friendly greeting, looking gentle and unassuming, and then suddenly they would throw the handkerchief noose round the neck of the wayfarer, strangle him in a moment, and rifle him of all he possessed. Sometimes a girl appeared sitting at the wayside weeping. The traveller, in pity, might stop to speak to her; but if so he was doomed. She soon had the noose round his throat, and strangled him on the spot. Since 1830 Thuggism has been suppressed, but the instinct possesses the thieves still, and the sight of the noose will cause the calm features to blaze with fury. In the school of industry at Jabalbur, some aged Thugs, proud of their race and profession, may still be seen. A visitor, anxious to understand their mode of strangling, submitted his neck to be operated upon, but at the great risk of his life; for with the kindling instinct of the Thug, the illustration threatened in another moment to become a reality. Datura poisoning is still practised by the same class of people. An old man and his son were lately poisoned for the sake of a new blanket by a gang of Thugs. The railroad now conveys us in ease and security over these vast plains."

The introduction of steam locomotion has greatly lessened the perils of travelling in India, and the stranger, under the protection of the railroad officials, feels pretty safe as he penetrates the interior. There are some novel features to the railway travelling, and more or less ludicrous incidents are met with, as well as many strange people.

The native population does not furnish a very attractive subject for speculation. The people are generally poor, and live on a sum that an American would think ridiculously small. How it is done, a person with a good appetite can hardly discover.

Calcutta has four hundred and fifty thousand inhabitants, and with its suburbs eight hundred and fifty thousand. It was located about two hundred years ago by Job Charnock, who went out as an agent of the East India Company. It has grown rapidly to power and influence. Its public buildings are elegant and commodious, and an American feels quite at home, as there are many American and English residents. The government houses, the Catholic and Protestant churches, the colleges and other edifices give the place a decidedly European aspect. It has been called "the city of palaces," and to some extent deserves the name. There are several newspapers printed in the English language, and some in the native languages, among the latter the *Poono Chundroday* (Rise of the Moon,) and the *Samachar Soodhaburshan* (Diffuser of Sweet News,) both of which are issued daily. Several colleges of influence and character show that the influences of education are prized in India as well as in America. The beneficent work of the missionaries is seen in Calcutta, as perhaps nowhere else in British India.

You may ask me something about the East India Company to which I have alluded. From a very early period the European power has had more or less control in India. The Portuguese and the Dutch were powerful in that country in the sixteenth century. When the English obtained power, a grant was given to what is known as the East India Company, to engage in trade, and in time, the Company became the representative of government, and able to defy it. The natives opposed the English as they had the Portuguese, and resisted the Company. In 1709 "The United Company of Merchants of England, trading in the East Indies," loaned the state £3,190,000 in consideration of the privilege of exclusive trade from the Cape of Good Hope to the Straits of Magellan. This company in some of its forms had existed since 1599, it received its charter from Elizabeth in 1600, but its power was not extensive until British rule made it an armed political engine of immense influence. It is a stock company, and while it has done much to open India to the rest of the world, and destroy its abominable superstitions, it has also done much to oppress the people. The name of Warren Hastings will suggest a history which one can hardly read without a blush. The opium trade, conducted by this company under the authority of the British government, has disgraced that government so that all the waters of the Ganges cannot wash out the stain.

RAILWAY TRAVELLING.

The extensive provinces of the British in India are now generally well governed, and Queen Victoria, in addition to the titles she derives from the English throne, bears the august title of " Empress of India." There have been twenty-eight governor-generals under the British crown, from Lord Clive, appointed in 1765, to the Marquis of Ripon, appointed in 1880; including Warren Hastings, Lord Cornwallis, Earl Canning and Lord Lytton. The British supremacy in India has not been altogether satisfactory to the rest of the world; but better perhaps than might be expected under the circumstances. The country has had its Buddhist period, its Mohammedan period, and its European period,—may we not hope to say, in time, its Christian period? The Hindus have made many efforts to cast off European rule, but without success, and never will until India has so far been enlightened as to become capable of self-government, and that day may be nearer than many suppose. The revolution of human thought in India is wonderful.

SERAMPORE.

This small city of less than twenty thousand inhabitants, situated about a dozen miles from Calcutta, is a charming place, on the right bank of the Hoogly. This place was one of the earliest scenes of missionary labors in India. William Carey, whose tomb is here, came from England in 1792. He was a wonderful man. At home he had been a shoemaker, but conceived the plan of converting India to Christianity. He translated the Bible into Bengali, and at Serampore founded a church and school, connected with which was a printing press. From this press came twenty-four different translations of the Scriptures, all of which he edited. He was one of the most remarkable Oriental scholars of modern times. The place is now a principal seat of Christian Missions.

ALDEEN.

This is a pilgrim spot, for here was the home of Henry Martyn, and the house in which he lived still stands. I would have every

MARTYN'S HOUSE, ALDEEN.

boy of the Triangle company read the Life of Martyn. Mrs. Sherwood, who knew him in India, describes him thus, — "He was dressed in white, and looked very pale, which, however, was nothing singular in India. His hair, a light brown, was raised from his forehead, which was a remarkably fine one. His features were not regular, but the expression was so luminous, so intellectual, so affectionate, so beaming with divine charity, that no one could have looked at his features and thought of their shape and form; the out-beaming of his soul would absorb the attention of every observer."

Lord Macaulay pays a beautiful tribute to his memory in these words: —

> "Here Martyn lies! In manhood's early bloom
> The Christian hero found a pagan tomb.
> Religion, sorrowing o'er her favorite son,
> Points to the glorious trophies which he won —
> Eternal trophies, not with slaughter red,
> Not stained with tears by hopeless captives shed.
> But trophies of the Cross; for that dear name
> Through every form of danger, death and shame,
> Onward he journeyed to a happier shore,
> Where danger, death, and shame are known no more."

The river Ganges, of which the Hoogly is a branch, is the principal river of India. It rises among the Himalaya mountains and flows down to the bay of Bengal. Its total length is about fifteen hundred miles. It is regarded by the Hindoos as a sacred stream, and many a mother has come and cast her babe into its waters as a religious act, and seen the defenceless little one crushed and broken between the jaws of some enormous crocodile that was waiting for such a victim. The river is to the Hindoos very much what the Nile is to the Egyptians. The country along the banks of the Ganges is wonderfully fertile, and the scenery remarkably beautiful. The boats are seen going up and down, filled with freight, while along the bank runs the East India Railway, more than nine hundred miles, and riding over it is much easier than going on the back of an elephant, or in a cart drawn by an ox.

The Himalaya mountains are to India what the Rocky mountains are to our own country. The ascent of the lofty peaks has all the charm that attends the ascent of Mount Washington, or climbing the ice-clad summits of the Alps. "Rising one morning while it was

yet dark," says a traveller, "we mounted our ponies, and, with guides, started for the ascent of the Sinchal Mountain (eight thousand three hundred feet), six miles from Darjeeling. Riding through the military sanatorium to 'the Saddle,' or Johr Bungalow, we began the ascent of a steep winding track through the jungle, and after an hour's climb reached the Chimneys — the ruins of the first military station — perched upon a ridge or shoulder of Sinchal, where Kinchinjunga and its

ON THE WAY TO THE HIMALAYAS.

neighbor peaks burst on our view, kindled with the rays of the rising sun. The air was perfectly clear, and the sky cloudless. Here we dismounted, and scrambled through brushwood and snow to the summit, which is specially celebrated, because of the glorious prospect it commands — the sweep of the Himalayan range, including Everest itself, the presiding monarch of them all, the highest mountain in the world. There he rose to our view, of sugar-loaf shape, far off, but clear cut against the sky. The entire range 'Pelion on Ossa piled,' was now before us as far as the eye could reach in a clear atmosphere and a cloudless sky. It was like looking from a Pisgah across the valleys and over mountains to a new and loftier country. Here one is overwhelmed with the majesty of Nature and the power of the Almighty. The deep blue sky, the pure white snows, the clear-cut precipices, the dark, shady ravines, the dense primeval forests, all impress the spectator with the presence of God."

BENARES.

We are now in the Mecca of India, the holy city, as sacred to the Hindoos as Jerusalem is to the Jews. The objects of interest are very numerous, — the Durga Temple, the Dasasamed Ghat, the Burning Ghat where the bodies of the dead are burned; the well of Vishnu or the well of Salvation, said to be filled with sweat from Vishnu's pores; the golden temple of Sivi, the special divinity of Benares; the Dhamek or tope, an immense building, built by King Asoka long before Christ, in which once stood eight elegant statues of Buddha, representing him in different characters; with many other things of note and much interest. All through the city, and at Sarnath, four miles to the northwest, are many remains of Buddhist worship and Buddhist splendor. Hindoo temples and the repulsive Brahmins are seen in all the streets, and the innumerable evidences of idolatry and heathenism meet the eye in all directions. The houses of the missionaries are found close to the temples of heathenism. The city is a fascinating one, and all the styles of Hindoo life are seen in the crowded habitations and on the banks of the river, where many of the people are engaged in various occupations.

BENARES.

LUCKNOW.

Lucknow has an interest quite different from that which enchains us at Benares. It is a city of three hundred and twenty thousand inhabitants, and has much natural and architectural beauty. The most conspicuous object is the great Imambara, in the fort, an immense structure, which the people regard as the central attraction of their city. The Dilkusa Palace, famous as having been the home of Sir Colin Campbell during the siege, is a fine building, but more

PAVILION OF TINKA, KAISER BAGH, LUCKNOW.

noted for its surroundings, the elegant park and garden, than for its own beauty. Everywhere about are evidences and mementoes of the siege. It was at Lucknow that the fearful mutiny of 1857 broke out, and marks of its atrocities are seen on every side. In one place stands the Residency, now in ruins, where Sir Henry Lawrence gathered the English women and children, and defended them for several months, losing his own life in his fidelity to the helpless creatures who fled to him for protection. In another place we are pointed to the garden where the English troops slaughtered two thousand Sepoys in revenge for the dreadful injury done to the British residents. Martinière is a group of palaces erected by Claude Martin, an eccentric Frenchman who came to India many years ago, and accumulated a vast fortune under the native government. The proprietor, when his huge building was finished, and covered with all sorts of ornaments, concluded that he did not want a palace, and turned the building into a school, and it now stands as his monument. The government elephant stables, where a hundred of these huge animals are kept, would interest the boys of the Triangle, I know. The Indian princes keep a large number of elephants for private and public use. Some of them become objects of much public regard and are treated as kindly as Jumbo, the elephant that has so long been known to boys and girls in English parks, but has now been sold to an American showman. I noticed not long ago in the "Indian Herald," a statement that "His sublime grandeur, the court and body elephant of the king of Siam," had just died, and that paper says, — "We regret to learn that the animal departed this life in a highly sensational manner, fraught with irreparable disaster to the staff of the household. One morning, after a hearty breakfast, he went mad quite unexpectedly, and trampled five of his attendants to death. To shoot him would have been sacrilege. An attempt to tranquillize his perturbed spirit by encircling him with a huge ring of holy bamboo, especially blessed by the high priest of his own particular temple, proved worse than ineffectual, for he broke through the ring and all but terminated the high priest's career upon the spot. He was then with great difficulty driven into a close court of the palace, where, after several furious endeavors to batter down the walls with his tusks, he suddenly toppled over on his side and uttered a last cry of rage. Naturally enough, this heavy calamity is attributed to carelessness on the part of one or other of the attendants entrusted with the sacred elephant's feeding. The king thereupon interrogated the members of his sublime grandeur's household in

STATE ELEPHANTS.

person with respect to treatment of the illustrious deceased, and failing to elicit any individual confession of delinquency, decreed that they should one and all be punished. Having thus vindicated propriety, his majesty assumed the garb of woe, and is understood to be still inconsolable for his loss."

The principal bazaar, the Chowk, is attractive to strangers, and is crowded all day long by all sorts and classes of people. On the whole, Lucknow is the most interesting Indian city I have seen. It is the capital of Oudh, and derives from the river Gumti much of its beauty.

ALAMBAGH.

One of the greatest generals England has ever had at the head of her armies was Henry Havelock, knighted for his valor at Lucknow. His name stands on the highest roll of fame. In Trafalgar Square a fine monument stands to his memory. But here where he fell is also a monument to speak his virtues. The monument in Trafalgar Square was erected by the British people. The monument here was erected by his widow and children. He was a noble Christian man. He said to General Outram just before he died, — "Outram, for more than forty years I have so ruled my life, that when death came, I might face it without fear." When the news of his death went back to England, there was unusual mourning, from the palace of the Queen to the humblest cottage in the land. The inscription on the monument is simple but true, — "He showed how the profession of a Christian could be combined with the duties of a soldier." This tomb will make Alambagh a pilgrim shrine as long as gratitude fills the British heart.

CAWNPORE.

It is but a short ride from Lucknow to this place. And here, too, you are in the midst of the relics of mutiny and massacre. The town has about one hundred thousand inhabitants. Here in 1857 was a force of three thousand eight hundred men, three thousand six hundred of whom were natives. When the mutiny broke out, Sir Hugh Wheeler, the commandant, defended himself as well as he could, but the natives all left him with his little force of European troops, and after a heroic struggle he was obliged to surrender. This he did, on the pledge that he should be allowed to have free passage to Allahabad. But as soon as he exposed his men to the enemy the bloodthirsty Sepoys, with Nena Sahib at their head, shot them down without mercy. For a time the women and children were spared, but on hearing of the rapid advance of General Havelock, the wretch who held their fate in his hands ordered them to be slain. Without mercy they were murdered and their bodies thrown into a well, which is now the first place visited by a European in Cawnpore. When the war was over, a memorial statue was placed over this well. It is an angel, with her arms folded on her breast, her wings thrown back, as she leans against the cross which is her support Her hands grasp a cluster of palm-leaves, while the monument

INDIAN FAKIR.

bears the inscription, — "Sacred to the perpetual memory of a great company of Christian people — chiefly women and children — who, near this spot, were cruelly massacred by the followers of the rebel Nena Dhoondopunt of Bithoor, and cast, the dying with the dead, into the well below, on the fifteenth day of July, 1857."

The city is largely engaged in manufactures of various kinds. The usual characters familiar in Indian cities are seen in the streets. The mendicant seeking your charity, and the fakir, or Mohammedan monk, the representative of a class of hermits who subject themselves to great austerities, and are held in high estimation as persons of peculiar devoutness and piety, after the manner of the country.

AGRA.

Within this city, or a few miles from it, are some of the most noted buildings in India. The Pearl Mosque, the fort at Agra, the palace, with the Panch Mahal at Futtepore Sikri, a short distance away, and other edifices draw the attention of all travellers. Of this Pearl Mosque, I would like to speak to you in the language of another, who says, — " Pre-eminent in beauty, within the fort of Agra is the Mutee Mosjid, or Pearl Mosque, also built by Shah Jehan, two hundred and forty feet from east to west, and one hundred and ninety feet from north to south, with an open court one hundred and fifty feet square. This building is wholly of white marble, from the pavement to the summit of its domes. The western part or mosque proper, is also of white marble, except an Arabic inscription from the Koran in black. The domes tower high above the other buildings of the fort, and in the glare of the morning sun look as if really built up of pearl. It is not only the Pearl Mosque, it is the pearl of mosques, unequalled in beauty by any other. But to all this white marble there is a dark side, 'dark scenes in the shades below balancing the brilliant scenes in the heights above. Deep down are seen mysterious stairs descending into empty cells and covered vaults, and from these again descending deeper and deeper still, through tortuous passages, ending apparently in nothing, yet with more than a suspicion of a something beyond, although a built-up wall interposes.

We examined these mysterious and dim retreats, and we saw enough to convince us that pleasure and pain, 'lust and hate,' were near neighbors in Agra, as in other places. Sad evidences were apparent of beings who from jealousy, or other causes, had been conveyed to these chambers of horror, and there executed in the eye of God

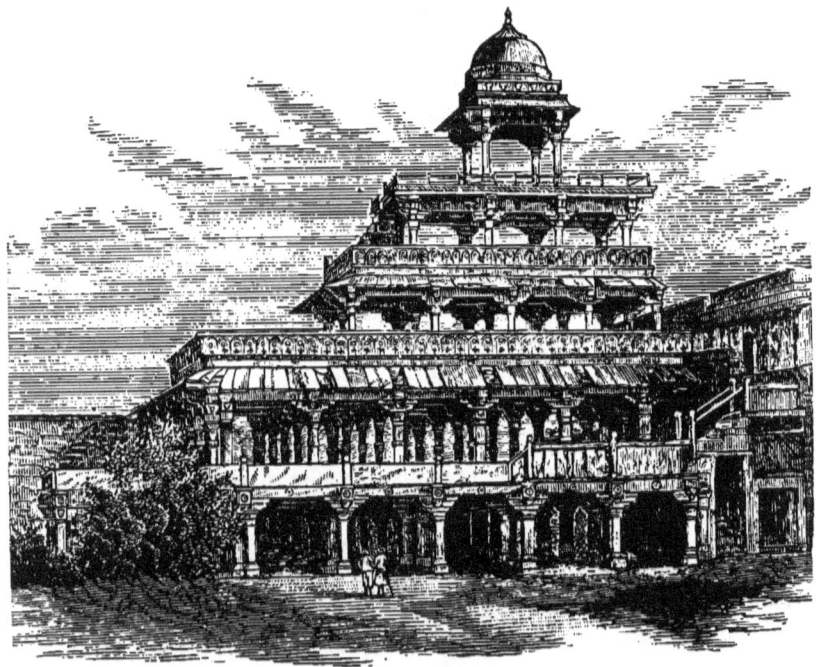

PANCH MAHAL, FUTTEPORE SIKRI.

alone. Beyond some of these barriers human skeletons have been found, some hung with ropes. Thus, side by side with the relics of Oriental splendor, are the visible tokens of Mogul cruelty."

But what is it, fact or imagination, that is so suggestive to us of crime and dark deeds, as we enter the elaborate edifices of the Hindus! No matter how elegant they are, or how sun-lighted they may be, they have the shadow of dark deeds pressing down upon them, and most of them are associated with crimes that have shocked the civilization of the whole world.

DELHI.

We are now in the "Punjaub." Well, you boys ask, "What is the 'Punjaub?'" I will tell you. India is divided, for the sake of good government, under British rules, into three presidencies,— Ben-

JUMMA MUSJID, DELHI.

gal, Madras, and Bombay. The Punjaub,— country of the five rivers, the rivers being Jhylum, Ravee, Beas, Sutlej, and Chenaub,— is a section in the northwestern part of the country, under a lieutenant-governorship, and is the least accessible part of the great empire. The city of Delhi is eight hundred and fifty miles from Calcutta, but easily reached by railway trains. It is a walled city, and has a population of one hundred and fifty thousand souls. It is on the river Jumna, and was one of the centres of war during the dreadful mutiny in 1857. Some of the most bloody scenes of the Sepoy war took place in this city. Here the sons of the king were exhibited after their execution, and the Chandi Chowk, — the bazaar street, — is full of memorial spots from which the blood seems hardly to be washed away.

Near Delhi is the famous fluted iron column, — the renowned Kuteer Minar. It is two hundred and forty feet high, and about one hundred feet in circumference near the ground. It was built about the year 1210, but little seems to be known about it. The carved columns of which it is composed are of iron, and taper to the top. From its summit a grand view is obtained.

Delhi is well provided with public inns, railway facilities, water privileges, and all the accessories of a great East Indian city. The Mohammedan population are as strict in their devotions, and as dishonest in their practices as elsewhere in the empire, and one has little to chose between them and the Buddhists. The Christian religion has quite a hold at Delhi. Various sects of Christians have planted monasteries and schools; churches and other religious institutions are found. The traveller in India always knows when he is near the seat of operation of Christian missionaries. The Gospel leaves its marks on all forms of society.

LAHORE.

The city is on the east bank of the river Ravee, and has a population of about one hundred thousand persons. There is not much to attract a stranger. It is a Hindu city, and all their cities are so much alike, that but for a few public buildings, and the local scenery, a description of one would do for all the rest. The life, the habits, the customs of the people, the religious institutions are the same, — the Mohammedan and Brahmin. Lahore has an elegant mosque of red stone built by Aurungzebe, a vernacular college, conducted by the English and supported by the government, with various buildings of more or less interest. It is the capital of the Punjaub, and as such, has an importance which it would not have under other circumstances.

HALL OF PRIVATE AUDIENCE, DELHI.

AMRITSAR.

Two hours' ride from Lahore brings you into Amritsar. If you want to know how Cashmere shawls are manufactured you can see it, for that branch of industry is carried to great perfection here. If you

TOMB OF RUNGIT-SING, LAHORE.

want to see all kinds of curious and wonderful ivory work, you can find it, for the workshops are busy with this kind of artistic manufacturing. If you want to see how low the human mind can be debased by idolatry, you can see it here, for the only God that a large part of the population know anything about is the "cow," a sacred animal that is held in more veneration than many people hold their Maker. If you want to see one of the most wonderful religious

GOLDEN TEMPLE OF THE SIKHS.

houses in the world, you will find it in this place, for the Golden Temple of the Sikhs (a religious brotherhood existing in this part of India, that reverence, if not worship the cow), is one of the most gorgeous buildings in the East. It is built of white marble, in the midst of an artificial lake, and its foundations are washed by the waters that shine and glisten all around it. A well-paved way leads

FLOATING GARDENS, LAKE OF SRINAGUR.

to the temple, on each side of which are statues, pillars, and lamps. The copper roof is gilded and shines like burnished gold. The windows have a golden hue. The silver doors turn easily on their hinges, and almost dazzle you as you approach. The floors are tesselated marble, rich mosaic work inlaid with many precious and rare stones. Language is inadequate to describe the effect of this elegant structure. It is no wonder that the citizens take great pride in it. Its watery surroundings do not a little to enhance its attractiveness.

At Srinagur, a place to which many resort for health, is a lake on which are found floating gardens, but I could not visit it at this time.

SIMLA.

We are now in what may be called the higher regions of India. What the Lebanon regions are to Syria, and the Alpine scenery is to Italy, this region is to Hindostan. The snow-clad ranges of mountains are not far distant, and the bracing air, the almost intoxicating winds, are full of life and energy. The whole region is one of great beauty, fully justifying the enthusiasm of an enthusiastic traveller, who exclaims, — "What with graceful deodaras, firs, oaks, rhododendrons, the magnificent scenery and the snow panorama, Simla is exceedingly beautiful. The rain and mist in June and July are dismal in the extreme; but from October the weather is enchanting. Simla is the seat of the Supreme Government for half the year, 'where it slumbers with a revolver under its pillow;' and it is therefore a place full of caste and cost, a sort of Indian Olympus, from whose heights the officials living at government expense look down with disdain upon the toilers in the plains beneath. It may be called a third heaven of flirtation and fashion. Indeed, one part is called Elysium. It is, as we say, 'out of the world;' but it seems when you get there as if the world with its pomps and vanities, had been caught up hither out of the world. It is an Indian Capua. You look over a billowy sea of hills to the great snowy range fifty miles away, its icy pinnacles glistening in the silent air as far as the eye can reach. The bazaar slopes gradually down the valley."

The shops of Simla are wonderfully attractive. Bric-a-brac of all descriptions is found in them, fancy articles, as well as useful things are shown, such as no country but India can exhibit. Much to our comfort, the weather is changing, and we have the best opportunity to see all the objects of interest. Each morning we say to each other, — "Is not this a charming day?" and yet each one seems to surpass the last.

However, we shall soon turn from the mountains toward the sea,

SHOPS. SRINAGUR KASHMIR.

although we have seen so much of India as to be bewildered, we seem hardly to have become acquainted with it.

The hot weather makes us wish to get into a cooler climate, or be nearer the sea. Chambers' Journal well describes the hot weather of India, — "say at a central position like Allahabad. In January the indoor temperature will reach its mininum, perhaps standing at fifty-four degrees. The rise is very gradual, and gets into the 'eighties' toward the middle of March; when steady at eighty-five degrees punkahs become necessary. Above ninety degrees the heat is oppressive, and at ninety-five degrees horribly so. This is generally the temperature indoors during the lull between the monsoons. In exceptional years I have known pillows and sheets to be uncomfortably hot, requiring sprinkling with water; and I have similarly retired to rest in drenched night-clothes. But the hot weather is mercifully interrupted by two remarkable meteorological phenomena. First, at its commencement we have almost always violent hail-storms, which beneficially cool the air, and then at its acme we have those very remarkable electrical dust-storms which impress fresh life and vigor all around. Let me describe one. Nature seems subdued under the great heat, and is in absolute repose. Not the faintest movement in the leaves; silence prevails, for even the garrulous crows can't caw because their beaks are wide open to assist respiration. Suddenly the welcome cry is heard, a storm coming! and the house servants rush in to close all doors. Anxious to witness the magnificence of the approaching storm you remain out to brave it, and soon feel its approaching breath on your cheek. Looking to windward you see a black cloud approaching, and before it leaves and sticks, kites and crows circling in wild confusion. You now hear its roar, and, while rapt in admiration, you are enveloped in its grimy mantle, and have to look to your footing in resisting its fury; and this is no joke, for eyes, nostrils, and ears are occluded with dust. As the blast approaches you may see a flash of lightning and hear its clap of thunder, and then feel the heavy cold rain-drops which sparsely fall around. Darkness, black as Erebus, surrounds you, darkness which literally may be felt, for clouds of dust occasion it; and if you are within doors, night prevails, requiring the lighting of lamps. The storm passes, light returns, and you find everything begrimed with dust. Every door is now thrown open to admit the cool, bracing, ozone-charged air, which you eagerly inhale with dilated nostrils, and feel that you have secured a fresh lease of existence." The punkahs referred to are the machines for fanning the rooms, which, in the hottest weather, need to be kept in motion continually.

CUTTACK.

Well, the time has come for me to leave India. From the Punjaub to Cuttack in the Bengal Presidency was quite a jump. It took many days, and many modes of travel, and many a weary ride to make it. Returning from the north, our company repaired to Allahabad, where, for reasons which I need not detail, our party broke up, some going to Bombay, which is about eight hundred and fifty miles in one direction, and Calcutta, which is far away in another. One of my friends, however, having decided to cross the Bengal Presidency to this point, I concluded to join him. We have come partly by rail, partly on elephants, partly in boats, and had a wild trip, and a fine chance to see the life of Indian towns that lie away from the main routes of travel. This town, the capital of a little province that bears the same name, is hardly worth a description, and I am only stopping here long enough to rest, in order to start again.

I propose to cross the Bay of Bengal, and proceed through Burmah and Siam into China. I shall wait here until some friends whose acquaintance I have made in India, arrive, when, with them, I shall proceed toward the Celestial empire.

RIP VAN WINKLE.

www.ingramcontent.com/pod-product-compliance
Lightning Source LLC
Chambersburg PA
CBHW030746250426
43672CB00028B/1106